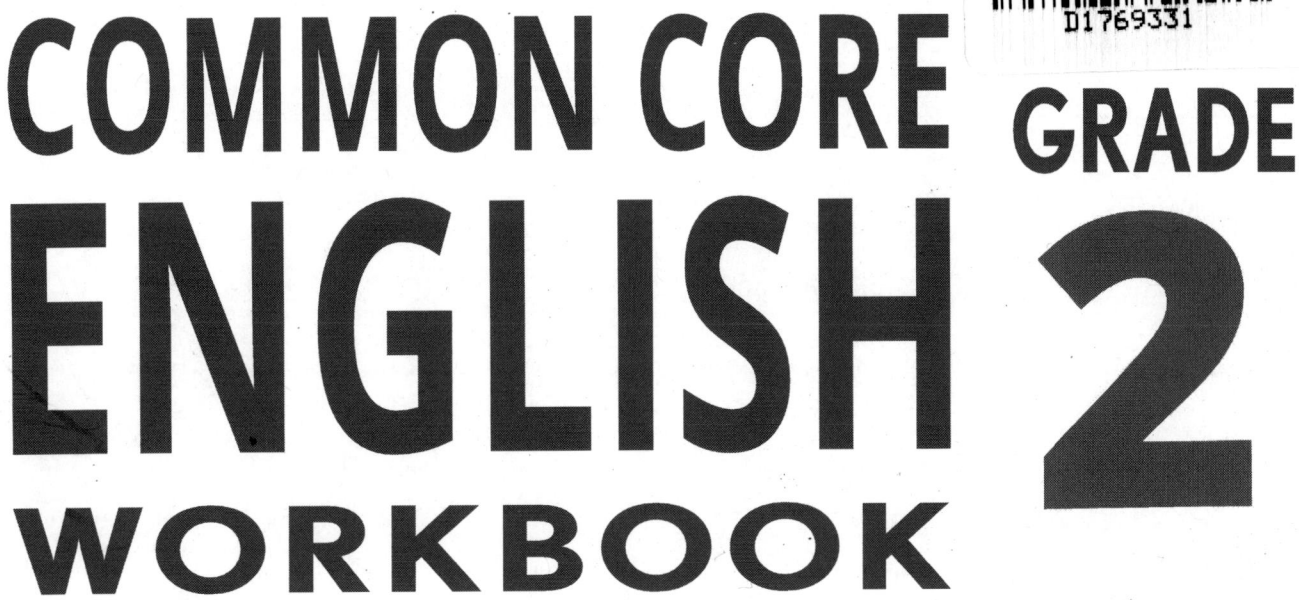

COMMON CORE ENGLISH WORKBOOK
GRADE 2

prepaze

www.prepaze.com

Author: Ace Academic Publishing

Ace Academic Publishing is a leading supplemental educational workbook publisher for grades K-12. At Ace Academic Publishing, we realize the importance of imparting analytical and critical thinking skills during the early ages of childhood and hence our books include materials that require multiple levels of analysis and encourage the students to think outside the box.

The materials for our books are written by award winning teachers with several years of teaching experience. All our books are aligned with the state standards and are widely used by many schools throughout the country.

Prepaze is a sister company of Ace Academic Publishing. Intrigued by the unending possibilities of the internet and its role in education, Prepaze was created to spread the knowledge and learning across all corners of the world through an online platform. We equip ourselves with state-of-the-art technologies so that knowledge reaches the students through the quickest and the most effective channels.

For inquiries and bulk orders, contact Ace Academic Publishing at the following address:

Ace Academic Publishing
3736 Fallon Road #403
Dublin CA 94568

www.aceacademicpublishing.com

This book contains copyright protected material. The purchase of this material entitles the buyer to use this material for personal and classroom use only. Reproducing the content for commercial use is strictly prohibited. Contact us to learn about options to use it for an entire school district or other commercial use.

ISBN: 978-1-949383-08-9

© Ace Academic Publishing, 2020

INTRODUCTION

About the Book

The content of the book includes multiple chapters and units covering all the required common core standards for the grade level. Similar to a standardized exam, you can find questions of all types - Multiple Choice, Fill in the blanks, True or False, Match the correct answer and Explain your Answers. The carefully chosen reading comprehension passages will help the students gain key comprehension skills such as themes, understanding figurative languages, character traits, and contextual vocabulary. The questions also cover writing standards that are not covered by most of the other commonly available workbooks. The exercises help students learn proper language convention and effectively use resources to research topics for writing essays. The detailed answer explanations help the students make sense of the problems and gain confidence in solving similar problems.

For the Parents

This workbook includes practice questions and tests that cover all the required Common Core Standards for the grade level. The book comprises multiple tests for each topic area so that your child can retake another test on the same topic. The workbook also includes questions for the writing standards and teaches your kid how to write essays and free responses. The workbook is divided into chapters and units so that you can choose the topics that you want your child to practice. The detailed answer explanations will teach your child the right methods to solve the problems for all types of questions, including the free-response questions. After completing the tests on all the chapters, your child can take any common core standardized exam with confidence and can excel in it.

For additional online practice, sign up for a free account at www.aceacademicprep.com.

For the Teachers

All questions and tests included in the Workbook are based on the core state standards and includes a clear label of the standard name. By following the chapter by chapter units, you can assign your students tests on a particular topic. The Workbook will help your students overcome any deficiencies in their understanding of critical concepts and will also help you identify the specific topics that may require more practice. The grade-appropriate, yet challenging questions will help your students learn to strategically use appropriate tools and persevere through common core standardized exams.

For additional online practice, sign up for a free account at www.aceacademicprep.com.

Other books from Ace Academic Publishing

Ace Academic Publishing
ACHIEVING EXCELLENCE TOGETHER

TABLE OF CONTENTS GRADE 2

1. **READING: LITERATURE**
   - 1.1. **KEY IDEAS AND DETAILS** 8
     Story Details • Central Theme • Character Development
   - 1.2. **CRAFT AND STRUCTURE** 20
     Understanding vocabulary • Story structure • Narrator's point of view
   - 1.3. **INTEGRATION OF KNOWLEDGE AND IDEAS** 31
     Story moods and illustrations • Compare/contrast story elements
   - 1.4. **CHAPTER REVIEW** 39

2. **READING: INFORMATIONAL TEXT**
   - 2.1. **KEY IDEAS AND DETAILS** 56
     Text details • Main idea • Sequence
   - 2.2. **CRAFT AND STRUCTURE** 64
     Understanding vocabulary • Locate information • Author's point of view
   - 2.3. **INTEGRATION OF KNOWLEDGE AND IDEAS** 73
     Visual illustrations • Text connections • Compare/contrast key details
   - 2.4. **CHAPTER REVIEW** 86

3. **READING: FOUNDATIONAL SKILLS**
   - 3.1. **PHONICS AND WORD RECOGNITION** 100
     Long and short vowels • Spelling-sound • Prefixes and suffixes
   - 3.2. **CHAPTER REVIEW** 107

4. **WRITING**
   - 4.1. **TEXT TYPES AND PURPOSES** 116
     Opinion pieces • Informative/explanatory writing • Narrative writing
   - 4.2. **CHAPTER REVIEW** 127

5. **LANGUAGE**
   - 5.1. **CONVENTIONS OF STANDARD ENGLISH** 140
     Conventions of grammar • Conventions of punctuation • Conventions of spelling
   - 5.2. **KNOWLEDGE OF LANGUAGE** 144
     Conventions of speaking and writing
   - 5.3. **VOCABULARY ACQUISITION AND USE** 148
     Multiple meaning words • Word relationships and nuances
   - 5.4. **CHAPTER REVIEW** 152

END OF YEAR ASSESSMENT 158

ANSWER KEY 185

1. READING: LITERATURE

1.1. KEY IDEAS AND DETAILS — 8
- Story Details
- Central Theme
- Character Development

1.2. CRAFT AND STRUCTURE — 20
- Understanding vocabulary
- Story structure
- Narrator's point of view

1.3. INTEGRATION OF KNOWLEDGE AND IDEAS — 31
- Story moods and illustrations
- Compare/contrast story elements

1.4. CHAPTER REVIEW — 39

1. READING:LITERATURE

1.1. Key Ideas and Details

Common Core State Standards: CCSS.ELA-LITERACY.RL.2.1, CCSS.ELA-LITERACY.RL.2.2, CCSS.ELA-LITERACY.RL.2.3

Skills:

- Demonstrate the understanding of key details in a text
- Recount stories and determine their central message, lesson, or moral
- Describe how characters in a story respond to major events and challenges

> **Directions:** Read the passage and answer the questions below.

=== EXAMPLE ===

THE GOOSE THAT LAID THE GOLDEN EGGS

There once was a man who owned a wonderful goose. Every morning, the goose laid for him a big, beautiful egg — an egg made of pure, shiny, solid gold. Every morning, the man collected golden eggs. And little by little, egg by egg, he began to grow rich. But the man wanted more.

"My goose has all those golden eggs inside her," he kept thinking. "Why not get them all at once?"

One day he couldn't wait any longer. He grabbed the goose and killed her. But there were no eggs inside her!

"Why did I do that?" the man cried. "Now there will be no more golden eggs."

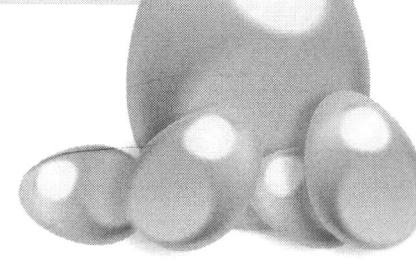

Copyrighted Material   www.prepaze.com

1. READING: LITERATURE

E1 **Why is the goose special?** (RL.2.1)
  A. The goose lays lots of eggs.
  B. The goose was expensive.
  C. The goose lays big eggs.
  D. The goose lays golden eggs.

Answer: D. The goose lays golden eggs.

E2 **Why did the man kill the goose?** (RL.2.2)
  A. For food
  B. For sport
  C. To get more eggs
  D. To look for gold

Answer: D. The man killed the goose because he thought it was illed with gold eggs.

E3 **How does the man feel after he kills the goose?** (RL.2.3)
  A. Excited
  B. Upset
  C. Happy
  D. Worried

Answer: B. The man is upset that he killed the goose.

1.1. KEY IDEAS AND DETAILS

1. READING: LITERATURE

> **Directions:** *Read the passage and answer the questions below.*

Fall Break Adventures

Normally, Ronald was cranky and groggy in the mornings. However, this was his fall break. He was happy to get up in the morning because he knew that he could do whatever he wanted to do. He didn't have to go school.

Ronald got ready for the day and went downstairs. Usually he hurries and grabs a granola bar for breakfast, but today his mother made him his favorite which is scrambled eggs and bacon.

"So, what do you want to do on your first day of fall break?" asked Ronald's mother.

" I want to go out to grandfather's woods and check the wilderness camera," said Ronald as he ate his scrambled eggs.

Ronald's yard touched his grandfather's yard. It was immense. Ronald and his mother got into their golf cart and rode over to grandfather's house. Ronald knocked on his grandfather's door.

"Hi grandpa! Do you want to go check the cameras?" said Ronald.

"Aren't you supposed to be in school little man?" joked Ronald's grandfather.

"Duh? It's fall break! Let's go!" said Ronald, impatiently waiting for his grandfather to put on his shoes.

Ronald's grandfather recently got a new wilderness camera. This is a special camera that takes pictures of animals in the daylight and at night. The camera automatically takes a picture when it senses movement.

When they got to the camera, Ronald's grandfather showed him how to take the camera off of the tree. He then showed him how to look at the photos. To their amazement, they saw a lot of nighttime activity. They saw deer, rabbits, racoons, the neighborhood cat, fox, coyotes, and a family of turkeys. From the camera, Ronald and his grandfather could see that the turkey nest was nearby.

"Wow! I didn't know there were turkey's here!" exclaimed Ronald.

"Yes, there are turkeys here sometimes. But unfortunately they get eaten every year by the coyotes," said Ronald's grandfather.

"Well, then let's do something about it," said Ronald.

...continued next page

1. READING: LITERATURE

> That afternoon, on Ronald's first day of fall break, Ronald and his grandfather got to work. They spent the entire day in his grandfather's shop. Ronald and his grandfather made a fence. When they finished, they put the fence around the turkey's nest on one side to keep away any large predators like coyotes.
>
> "Good job, Ronald! The turkeys thank you!" exclaimed grandfather. "How was your first day of fall break?"
>
> Ronald smiled and said, "Fabulous! What will we do tomorrow?"

FREE RESPONSE

1. **How was the problem in this passage solved?** (RL.2.1)

   _____
   _____
   _____
   _____
   _____

2. **Why did Ronald and his grandfather spend the afternoon building a fence?** (RL.2.1)

   _____
   _____
   _____
   _____
   _____

1.1. KEY IDEAS AND DETAILS

1. READING: LITERATURE

MULTIPLE CHOICE

3. What did Ronald see on the wilderness camera that concerned him? (RL.2.1)

A. Coyotes
B. Birds
C. Turkeys
D. Fox

4. What did Ronald do about this problem? (RL.2.1)

A. He built a fence to put around the turkey nest.
B. He made a trap for the coyotes.
C. He took copies of all the pictures on his grandfather's wilderness camera.
D. He went to see if the turkeys were in their nest.

FILL IN THE BLANK

5. How does Ronald see the turkeys and the other animals? He sees them on the _____. (RL.2.1)

TRUE OR FALSE

6. Ronald loves nature. (RL.2.1)

A. True
B. False

> **Directions:** Read the passage and answer the questions below.

A Tricky Monkey

Kojo, the monkey lived in the rainforest. There were lots of monkeys in Kojo's part of the forest. Kojo had many brothers and sisters. That was good because Kojo had many monkeys to play with. But Kojo liked to get attention, too. That was hard to do with so many monkeys around.

One day Kojo decided to play a trick on the other monkeys. "Leopard!" Kojo cried. "A leopard is coming!" The monkeys scrambled. They climbed up to the highest tree branches. They shook with fear. Leopards like to eat monkeys.

Kojo laughed. "Ha! Just kidding," he said. Kojo's Aunt Ama scolded him. "Nobody likes a liar, Kojo." Kojo felt bad for a little while. But he soon got bored. A few days later, he did it again.

...continued next page

1. READING: LITERATURE

"Leopard!" Kojo cried. "A leopard is coming!" The monkeys scrambled again. Kojo laughed. "Ha! Just kidding again," he said. Aunt Ama shook her head. "Be careful, Kojo. Nobody will believe anything you say if you keep this up." The monkeys were all pretty upset with Kojo. They ignored him. Kojo sat in a tree branch, bored and lonely.

Then he saw a shadow on the ground below. A hungry-looking leopard padded across the rainforest floor. "Leopard! A leopard is coming for real this time!" Kojo yelled. None of the monkeys paid any attention. The leopard was headed right for them. Kojo knew what he had to do.

"Here, leopard! Over here!" he yelled. The leopard chased Kojo. Kojo climbed up to the highest branches. The other monkeys now saw the leopard and they climbed into the trees, too. The leopard could not climb as high as the monkeys. She gave up and walked away.

Kojo was relieved. The other monkeys were glad that Kojo had tried to save them. They forgave him for lying and played with him again. And Kojo became someone they could trust.

1.1 KEY IDEAS AND DETAILS

FREE RESPONSE

7. What is the lesson in this story? (RL.2.2)

_____
_____
_____
_____

MULTIPLE CHOICE

8. Why did Kojo yell "leopard" the first time? (RL.2.2)

A. He saw a leopard.
B. He wanted to hurt his friends.
C. He wanted attention.
D. He was confused.

1. READING: LITERATURE

FILL IN THE BLANK

9. When Kojo called "leopard" the third time all of the monkeys _____. (RL.2.2)

10. Kojo earned back the monkeys' trust by trying to _____ them. (RL.2.2)

TRUE OR FALSE

11. Kojo distracted the leopard because he felt guilty for lying. (RL.2.2)

    A. True
    B. False

> **Directions:** Read the passage and answer the questions below.

THE LION AND THE MOUSE

A Lion lay asleep in the forest, his great head resting on his paws. A timid little Mouse came upon him unexpectedly, and in her fright and haste to get away, ran across the Lion's nose. Roused from his nap, the Lion laid his huge paw angrily on the tiny creature to kill her.

"Spare me!" begged the poor Mouse. "Please let me go and someday I will surely repay you."

The Lion was much amused to think that a Mouse could ever help him. But he was generous and finally let the Mouse go.

Some days later, while stalking his prey in the forest, the Lion was caught in the toils of a hunter's net. Unable to free himself, he filled the forest with his angry roar. The Mouse knew the voice and quickly found the Lion struggling in the net. Running to one of the great ropes that bound him, she gnawed it until it parted, and soon the Lion was free.

"You laughed when I said I would repay you," said the Mouse. "Now you see that even a Mouse can help a Lion."

1.1. KEY IDEAS AND DETAILS

1. READING:LITERATURE

FREE RESPONSE

12. What is the moral of the story? (RL.2.2)

_____

_____

_____

_____

13. Why did the Lion laugh when the Mouse offered to repay him? (RL.2.2)

_____

_____

_____

_____

14. How does the Lion change during the story? (RL.2.3)

_____

_____

_____

_____

1.1. KEY IDEAS AND DETAILS

1. READING:LITERATURE

15. What did the Mouse do when the Lion caught her? (RL.2.3)

_____

_____

_____

_____

_____

_____

_____

=== MULTIPLE CHOICE ===

16. Why did the Lion let the Mouse go? (RL.2.2)
  A. He wanted the Mouse to do something for him.
  B. He was generous.
  C. He was selfish.
  D. He was helpful.

17. Which word does not describe the Mouse in the story? (RL.2.3)
  A. Clever   B. Loyal   C. Timid   D. Angry

=== TRUE OR FALSE ===

18. The Mouse offered to help the Lion as a clever way to avoid being eaten. (RL.2.3)
  A. True   B. False

1.1. KEY IDEAS AND DETAILS

1. READING: LITERATURE

> **Directions:** *Read the passage and answer the questions below.*

Valentine's Day

Jackie is so excited because today is Valentine's Day. Her school allows the students to celebrate this holiday. She spent a lot of time making homemade Valentine's cards. Her dad and her also spent time making little goody bags with toys, candy, yo-yos, and silly putty. She closed the bags with a pretty red ribbon. Her dad drove her to school and helped her carry in her cards and gifts.

As Jackie walked into her classroom, she was so surprised. Her teacher, Mrs. Catchem, decorated the entire classroom with red streamers, hearts, and red balloons. It looked so nice.

After the morning bell and morning math work, it was time for their party. The teacher told the students to get out their Valentine's Day cards and get ready to pass them out. Jackie was getting her box out that she created to gather all of her cards. She looked beside her and saw Ezra with his head down. She shrugged and thought that he never paid attention to what the teacher said. Ezra just sat there with his head down on the desk. The teacher then announced that she will be calling out table numbers to pass out cards.

"Tables one and two, please" said Mrs. Catchem.

Jackie leaned over to Ezra. "Get out your cards, Ezra," she said to him. Ezra lifted his head, looked at her, and then sadly looked down at his feet. Oh, thought Jackie. She finally realized that Ezra didn't have any Valentine's cards.

"Tables three and four, please" announced Mrs. Catchem.

Table three is Jackie and Ezra's table. Jackie turned around quickly and put the box of gifts on Ezra's desk. She was happy that she didn't put her name on them. She said in a loud voice so all her classmates would hear, "Wow Ezra! These goody bags you made are great!"

Ezra was confused at first, but then he caught on. Ezra quickly got up out of his seat and passed out the goody backs to his classmates.

Later that day, she received a handwritten letter on red paper on her desk. She opened it up. It said, "Thanks for being a friend. Happy Valentine's Day. Love, Ezra."

1.1. KEY IDEAS AND DETAILS

1. READING: LITERATURE

FREE RESPONSE

19. Describe how Jackie responds to Ezra not having Valentine's Day cards. (RL.2.3)

1.1. KEY IDEAS AND DETAILS

1. READING: LITERATURE

20. How does Ezra's behavior change throughout the story? (RL.2.3)

_____

_____

_____

_____

_____

_____

_____

_____

_____

1.1. KEY IDEAS AND DETAILS

1.2. CRAFT AND STRUCTURE

NAME: _____ DATE: _____

1. READING: LITERATURE

1.2. Craft and Structure

Common Core State Standards: CCSS.ELA-LITERACY.RL.2.4, CCSS.ELA-LITERACY.RL.2.5, CCSS.ELA-LITERACY.RL.2.6

Skills:
- Describe how words and phrases supply rhythm and meaning in a story, poem, or song
- Describe the overall structure of a story
- Acknowledge differences in the points of view of characters

> **Directions:** *Read the passage and answer the questions below.*

EXAMPLE

> White sheep, white sheep,
> On a blue hill,
> When the wind stops,
> You all stand still.
> When the wind blows,
> You walk away slow.
> White sheep, white sheep,
> Where do you go?

E1 **Which of these words in the poem rhymes with the word *slow*?** (RL.2.4)
  A. go   **B.** still   **C.** sheep   **D.** stops

Answer: **A.** The word *go* rhymes with the word *slow*.

EXAMPLE

> On the first day of school, Carl was in a hurry. He wanted to get to his new classroom so that he could pick out his desk. Carl grabbed his lunch bag and threw it in his backpack. He quickly walked at a fast pace toward the school.

1. READING:LITERATURE

E2 **What does the beginning of the story tell you? Choose the best answer.** (RL.2.5)

   A. The story is about school.
   B. Carl is in a hurry to get to his new classroom.
   C. Carl made his lunch for school.
   D. Carl walked quickly toward the school.

Answer: **B.** The beginning of the story introduces the reader to Carl and lets the reader know that Carl is in a hurry to pick out his desk.

EXAMPLE

> "These cookies are gross!" said Patrick. "I hate raisins! Who puts raisins in cookies?"
>
> Amanda smiled at him and shook her head. "I love raisins!" she exclaimed. "Oatmeal raisin cookies are my favorite."

E3 **How are the two characters' points of view different?** (RL.2.6)

   A. They both like cookies.
   B. Only Patrick likes oatmeal raisin cookies.
   C. Both characters hate raisins.
   D. Patrick does not like raisins in cookies while Amanda loves them.

Answer: **D.** Based on the dialogue in the story, the reader knows that Patrick thinks raisins in cookies are gross, but Amanda says oatmeal raisin cookies are her favorite.

1.2. CRAFT AND STRUCTURE

1. READING: LITERATURE

> **Directions:** *Read the poem and answer the questions below.*

THE TERRIBLE THING ABOUT CINDY

The terrible thing about Cindy
Is she packs a powerful punch.
I learned this yesterday at school
When I tried to take her lunch.

I had only meant to tease her,
To make her squeal and twist.
The last thing I expected
was her calculated fist.

She socked me in the stomach –
She's more than slightly deft –
And sent me stumbling to my knees,
As she snatched her lunch and left.

After that, I was quite sorry
I had tussled with a pro –
I wish my friends had told me
That she practiced tae kwon do.

TRUE OR FALSE

1. **In the poem, Cindy punched someone trying to take her lunch.** (RL.2.4)

   A. True   **B.** False

2. **The word *squeal* means "to trip".** (RL.2.4)

   A. True   **B.** False

1. READING:LITERATURE

3. The words *socked* and *punch* have similar meanings. (RL.2.4)

　A. True　　　　　　　　　　**B.** False

4. The word *twist* rhymes with *fist*. (RL.2.4)

　A. True　　　　　　　　　　**B.** False

--- **FREE RESPONSE** ---

5. Who is the speaker of the poem? How do you know? (RL.2.4)

_____

_____

_____

_____

_____

6. How does the author of the poem feel about his or her actions? (RL.2.4)

_____

_____

_____

_____

_____

_____

_____

1. READING: LITERATURE

7. Why do you think the poem is titled "The Terrible Thing About Cindy"? (RL.2.4)

_____

_____

_____

_____

_____

_____

_____

_____

> **Directions:** *Read the passage and answer the questions below.*

Mason's Trip to New York City

Mason and his family took a trip to New York City. They traveled during their spring break vacation. The family packed their suitcases. They made sure to bring enough clothes for a four-day trip.

The family of five boarded an airplane. Mason's mom, dad, and baby sister sat in the first row. Mason and his big sister, Katie, sat in the second row of the airplane. Before the plane took off, Mason fell asleep. Within a few hours, the family arrived in New York City.

Mason was very excited to get to the hotel. He wanted to drop off his suitcase and start seeing the city. First, the family traveled to see the Statue of Liberty. The statue was so big up close! Mason and Katie took turns taking pictures of each other in front of the statue. The next day, the family went to the Empire State Building. They took an elevator

...continued next page

1. READING: LITERATURE

to the very top. Mason read about the history of the building. It used to be the tallest building in New York City. On the third day, the family walked to Times Square. There were so many people, stores, and restaurants nearby. On the last day of the trip, Mason and his family visited Central Park. Mason and Katie ran around the park. The family ate a picnic lunch before they went back to their hotel. They talked about all the places they had visited and everything they had seen. It was a great family vacation!

=== TRUE OR FALSE ===

8. Mason and his family traveled during March or April. (RL.2.5)

   A. True   **B.** False

9. The setting of the beginning of the story is on an airplane. (RL.2.5)

   A. True   **B.** False

10. The story takes place over four days. (RL.2.5)

   A. True   **B.** False

=== FREE RESPONSE ===

11. Who is telling the story? How do you know? (RL.2.5)

1.2. CRAFT AND STRUCTURE

1. READING: LITERATURE

1.2. CRAFT AND STRUCTURE

12. **Where does the story begin?** (RL.2.5)

_____
_____
_____
_____
_____
_____
_____

13. **How does the setting change throughout the story?** (RL.2.5)

_____
_____
_____
_____
_____
_____
_____
_____
_____
_____

1. READING:LITERATURE

14. How does the ending conclude the action of the story? (RL.2.5)

___

> **Directions:** Read the passage and answer the questions below.

Playing it Safe

Laura wanted to go on a bike ride, so she got her bike out of the shed and put on her pink bike helmet. Before she took off, Laura spotted her brother Tommy heading in her direction. He asked where she was going and told her he wanted to go, too. Laura invited him along for the bike ride. Tommy quickly grabbed his bike.

"Where is your helmet?" Laura asked him.

"I don't need it," Tommy answered. "I think it makes me look funny. Besides, it's uncomfortable to wear."

Laura did not think it was a good idea for Tommy to not wear his bike helmet, but she decided her brother could make his own choices. The pair started out on their bike ride ready for some adventure.

...continued next page

1. READING: LITERATURE

After riding for a while, Tommy said he wanted to lead the way. "Follow me!" he shouted to his sister. Laura followed Tommy down a dirt road that led them over quite a few big hills and under many tall trees. Tommy started to show off on his skills and began riding a little too fast.

"Slow down!" yelled Laura.

Tommy just ignored his sister and rode even faster. Soon he began to lose control of his bike, and he crashed! Tommy hit his leg on a big rock and bumped his head against a tree stump.

"Oh no!" cried Laura. She quickly rode over to her brother. Laura reached down and helped pull Tommy back up on his feet.

Tommy said he was very sorry. "You were right, sis," he sighed. "I guess I should have worn my bike helmet. I promise I will from now on."

1.2. CRAFT AND STRUCTURE

TRUE OR FALSE

15. Laura is telling the story from her point of view. (RL.2.6)

   A. True　　　　　　　　　B. False

16. Tommy did not practice bike safety. (RL.2.6)

   A. True　　　　　　　　　B. False

17. The story takes place outside. (RL.2.6)

   A. True　　　　　　　　　B. False

FREE RESPONSE

18. What could Tommy have done differently to change what happened to him in the story? (RL.2.6)

_____

_____

_____

_____

1. READING:LITERATURE

19. How do you think Laura was feeling when she saw Tommy riding too fast? (RL.2.6)

1.2. CRAFT AND STRUCTURE

1. READING: LITERATURE

20. Why do you think Tommy changed his point of view about wearing a bike helmet? (RL.2.6)

_____
_____
_____
_____
_____
_____
_____
_____
_____
_____

1.2. CRAFT AND STRUCTURE

1.3. INTEGRATION OF KNOWLEDGE AND IDEAS

NAME: _____ DATE: _____

1. READING: LITERATURE

1.3. Integration of Knowledge and Ideas

Common Core State Standards: CCSS.ELA-LITERACY.RL.2.7, CCSS.ELA-LITERACY.RL.2.9

Skills:
- Use information gained from the illustrations and words in a print or digital text to demonstrate an understanding of its characters, setting, or plot
- Compare and contrast two or more versions of the same story by different authors or from different cultures

> **Directions:** *Read the passage and answer the questions below.*

=== EXAMPLE ===

The ocean waves were tossing and turning. The wind was freezing cold. The sand felt cool to the touch. The wind picked up the sand and moved it up and down the coastline.

E1 Where is the specific setting of the story? (RL.2.7)

A. Outside
B. In the mountains
C. At the coast
D. During winter

Answer: C. Based on the descriptions in the text, the reader should identify the setting of the story at the coast.

=== EXAMPLE ===

STORY 1

Tyler sat down at his desk to take his test. As he wrote his name on the top of the paper, his pencil broke. He didn't know what to do next. He didn't have any extra pencils in his backpack.

...continued next page

1. READING:LITERATURE

STORY 2

Tyler sat down at his desk to take his test. As he wrote his name on the top of the paper, his pencil broke. A classmate saw what had happened and leaned over to give Tyler an extra pencil. "Thank you," Tyler said quietly.

E2 **How does the second story differ from the first story?** (RL.2.9)

- **A.** It has a different character.
- **B.** The pencil doesn't break.
- **C.** A classmate gives Tyler an extra pencil to use.
- **D.** Tyler doesn't take the test.

Answer: **C.** The reader should understand the difference between the two stories is that Tyler is given an extra pencil to use by a classmate.

> **Directions:** *Read the passage and answer the questions below.*

Summer Plans

It was the last day of school. Milo and his three friends sat outside eating their lunch. They became great friends this year in the second grade. They talked about their plans for the summer.

Milo was going to go to Florida. His parents had to work and they couldn't find a babysitter for him, so he was going to go down to Florida to stay with his grandmother. He was going to fly on a plane by himself. He was a little nervous about it, but knew he could do it. He said that his grandmother was very lonely. Milo looked forward to going on outings with her to the beach, to Disneyland, and to the zoo. He also looked forward to helping her and taking walks with her.

Milo's friend Oscar was not going too far from Indiana. He was going to Michigan. His parents rent a condo on Mackinac Island which is in Northern Michigan. They can't drive to the island, they have to take a ferry as there are no cars allowed. On the island, Oscar and his family will relax, swim in the lake, hike, and ride bikes. Oscar loves the fudge and taffy on the island and promised to bring back some treats for his friends when he returns.

...continued next page

1. READING:LITERATURE

Tanya was a bit jealous of Milo and Oscar as she was not going anywhere for summer vacation, but she did have plans. She was going to go to the Boys and Girls Club everyday. There, she would take walks, go on nature hikes, and go swimming at the public pool. Tanya was also going to go to summer school. She wanted to go to summer school because she struggled a bit during the year with math. She wanted to get ahead for the next year. Tanya was also looking forward to having cookouts with her dad.

Erica was going to do something a bit different. Her dad was a long distance semi-truck driver, and she didn't see her dad very much during the school year. So this summer, her and her dog are going to ride along in the truck with her dad. She will spend some time with her dad and see many different states. Her dad drives trucks from California all the way to New York. She was looking forward to seeing the different parts of the United States.

The four friends couldn't wait for their plans, and they couldn't wait until they were third graders. They looked forward to their first day of third grade to share their stories of the summer.

1.3. INTEGRATION OF KNOWLEDGE AND IDEAS

=== MULTIPLE CHOICE ===

1. **What is the plot of the story?** (RL.2.7)
   A. Four friends are spending their summer vacation together.
   B. Four friends are explaining their summer plans.
   C. One friend feels left out because she is not going anywhere for the summer.
   D. Four friends go swimming at the local pool.

1. READING:LITERATURE

2. **Who is telling the story?** (RL.2.7)
   A. Each of the four friends
   B. Oscar
   C. Milo
   D. An outside narrator

3. **What does the word *condo* mean?** (RL.2.7)
   A. A place to stay   B. An animal   C. A place to swim   D. School

4. **What was Milo slightly nervous about related to his summer plans?** (RL.2.7)
   A. Flying on a plane by himself
   B. Being stuck in a semi-truck for hours
   C. Going to summer school
   D. Swimming in the ocean with sharks

5. **Which two characters have similar plans of swimming in a natural body of water over the summer?** (RL.2.7)
   A. Milo and Oscar
   B. Oscar and Erica
   C. Erica and Tanya
   D. Milo and Erica

6. **What character will be staying in Indiana during the summer?** (RL.2.7)
   A. Milo   B. Oscar   C. Tanya   D. Erica

7. **How will the setting be different for Tanya in comparison to Erica?** (RL.2.7)
   A. Tanya's setting is Indiana and Erica's setting is Florida.
   B. Tanya's setting is Florida and Erica's setting is Indiana.
   C. Tanya's setting is Indiana and Erica's setting will be different states in the United States.
   D. Tanya's setting is Michigan and Erica's setting will be different states in the United States.

8. **If there was an illustration about Tanya's summer plans, what would the illustration be of?** (RL.2.7)
   A. A picture of Tanya in the classroom.
   B. A picture of Tanya swimming in a lake.
   C. A picture of Tanya on a plane.
   D. A picture of Tanya in a semi-truck.

1.3. INTEGRATION OF KNOWLEDGE AND IDEAS

1. READING: LITERATURE

9. **Which character will spend the least amount of time in a vehicle during their summer plans?** (RL.2.7)

   A. Milo   **B.** Oscar   **C.** Tanya   **D.** Erica

10. **Which character will most likely spend more time at an ocean?** (RL.2.7)

    A. Milo   **B.** Oscar   **C.** Tanya   **D.** Erica

> **Directions:** *Read the passages and answer the questions below.*

Sandra's Adventure Under the Sea

Sandra really loved fish. She planned to go scuba diving because she wanted to get a closer look at the fish under the sea. On the first day of summer, Sandra went out on a big boat. The boat took her to a deep part of the ocean. When the boat stopped, Sandra put on her scuba gear. She had been scuba diving before. She knew how to breathe correctly with the gear on. Sandra knew she had to slowly swim under the water and when to pop her ears.

When she was ready, she jumped out of the boat and made a big splash. She quickly kicked her legs and moved her arms. Sandra swam down many feet under the water. Along the way down, she saw colorful rocks, shells, and plants. Sandra saw lots of fish. She also saw an octopus, a jellyfish, and a brightly colored seahorse.

After a few minutes under the water, Sandra spotted a sea turtle heading in her direction. Her heart started racing. She was so excited! She loved sea turtles. Sandra wanted to take a picture with the turtle, so she grabbed her underwater camera. Sandra swam next to the sea turtle and then snapped a photo. She swam a few more feet down. After seeing more underwater creatures, Sandra was ready to go back to the boat. She slowly swam up to the surface of the water. When she climbed back onto the boat, she took off her gear. Sandra had a fun adventure under the sea!

1.3. INTEGRATION OF KNOWLEDGE AND IDEAS

1. READING: LITERATURE

Shane's Adventure Under the Sea

Shane really loved fish. He thought he should try scuba diving. He had never done it before. He was nervous to go but knew he could see the fish up close. On the last day of summer, Shane went out on a big boat. The boat took him to a deep part of the ocean. Shane got his scuba gear ready. Because he had never been diving before, he had to take a lesson on how to breathe correctly with the gear on. He was told he had to slowly swim under the water and when he had to pop his ears.

When he was ready, he swung his legs over the side of the boat. He made his way into the water and began kicking his legs and moving his arms. Shane began to panic. He had trouble with his gear, and it was hard for him to breathe. Shane tried to calm down and focus on his breathing by taking deep breaths. He was now ready to go under the water. He saw colorful seaweed and swam near a school of fish. He saw a stingray, a crab, and a brightly colored starfish.

After a few minutes under the water, Shane spotted a dolphin heading in his direction. He could not believe his eyes. He was so excited! Shane wanted to get closer to the dolphin. As he swam towards the dolphin, he could hear it making noises under the water. Before he got too close, the dolphin quickly swam away and was no longer in sight. Shane was ready to go back to the boat. When he climbed on board, he took off his gear. Shane had a fun adventure under the sea!

=== MULTIPLE CHOICE ===

11. What is the plot of both stories? (RL.2.9)
- **A.** Friends go scuba diving together.
- **B.** Scuba diving is dangerous.
- **C.** You can see many aquatic creatures under the sea when you scuba dive.
- **D.** Scuba diving is a fun adventure under the sea.

1. READING:LITERATURE

12. Who is telling both stories? (RL.2.9)
   A. Sandra
   B. Shane
   C. A scuba instructor
   D. The narrator

13. What did both characters do in the two stories? (RL.2.9)
   A. Both took a big boat to a deep part of the ocean.
   B. Both swam quickly through the water.
   C. Both saw seaweed.
   D. Both got sick.

14. What did both characters see under the water? (RL.2.9)
   A. Both saw a crab.
   B. Both saw a fish.
   C. Both saw starfish.
   D. Both saw turtles.

15. How is Sandra's scuba diving adventure similar to Shane's? (RL.2.9)
   A. Both had a fun adventure under the sea.
   B. Both had new diving gear to wear.
   C. Both saw the same types of fish under the water.
   D. Both went scuba diving again.

16. Why was it easier for Sandra to go scuba diving? (RL.2.9)
   A. She was smaller.
   B. She had been scuba diving before.
   C. She took lessons on how to breathe correctly.
   D. She was older.

17. Why would it be easier for Sandra to go scuba diving again during the summer? (RL.2.9)
   A. Because she didn't have a job
   B. Because school was out for the summer
   C. Because she went scuba diving on the first day of summer, not on the last day like Shane did
   D. Because she liked to scuba dive

1.3. INTEGRATION OF KNOWLEDGE AND IDEAS

1. READING:LITERATURE

18. **Why did Shane have trouble breathing underwater unlike Sandra?** (RL.2.9)
    A. Because his equipment was broken
    B. Because he had trouble with his gear
    C. Because he was scared
    D. Because this was his first-time scuba diving

19. **Which character saw more animals and plants underwater?** (RL.2.9)
    A. Sandra
    B. Shane
    C. It was equal
    D. I cannot tell from the text

20. **Overall, how do the two adventures under the sea compare?** (RL.2.9)
    A. They are very different.
    B. They are similar.
    C. They are exactly the same.
    D. I cannot tell from the text.

1.4. Chapter Review

1. READING: LITERATURE

1.4. Chapter Review

> **Directions:** *Read the passage and answer the questions below.*

THE LION AND THE MOUSE

A Lion lay asleep in the forest, his great head resting on his paws. A timid little Mouse came upon him unexpectedly, and in her fright and haste to get away, ran across the Lion's nose. Roused from his nap, the Lion laid his huge paw angrily on the tiny creature to kill her.

"Spare me!" begged the poor Mouse. "Please let me go and someday I will surely repay you."

The Lion was much amused to think that a Mouse could ever help him. But he was generous and finally let the Mouse go.

Some days later, while stalking his prey in the forest, the Lion was caught in the toils of a hunter's net. Unable to free himself, he filled the forest with his angry roar. The Mouse knew the voice and quickly found the Lion struggling in the net. Running to one of the great ropes that bound him, she gnawed it until it parted, and soon the Lion was free.

"You laughed when I said I would repay you," said the Mouse. "Now you see that even a Mouse can help a Lion."

=== **FREE RESPONSE** ===

1.   How does the Mouse help the Lion? (RL.2.1)

_____

_____

_____

_____

_____

1. READING: LITERATURE

MULTIPLE CHOICE

2. **What happened to the Lion?** (RL.2.1)
   - **A.** He was shot by a hunter.
   - **B.** He is caught in a net.
   - **C.** He is hurt in the forest.
   - **D.** He is angry and roaring.

TRUE OR FALSE

3. **The Mouse was amused because the Lion decided to help him.** (RL.2.1)
   - **A.** True
   - **B.** False

4. **The Mouse comes to save the Lion because she hears his roar.** (RL.2.1)
   - **A.** True
   - **B.** False

> **Directions:** *Read the passage and answer the questions below.*

THE CLASSROOM

Ms. Jones had seven students in her classroom. Kelly, Mark, and Josh sat in the front row. Jimmy, Hannah, Claire, and Abby sat in the back row. Each morning, the students would recite the alphabet. They would write down each letter in their notebooks.

Mark liked to race through the lesson and write down the letters as fast as he could. "I'm done, Ms. Jones," called Mark.

"I see that you wrote the letters down, but some of your handwriting is sloppy. You should write them again slowly," said Ms. Jones.

While Mark was working on correcting his mistakes, Jimmy threw a paper airplane at Mark's head. Hannah giggled.

Ms. Jones looked at her students seated in the back row. "Did you do that, Hannah?" asked Ms. Jones.

Hannah suddenly stopped giggling. Her face turned bright red. "Oh no, Ms. Jones! Jimmy did it. He threw the airplane at Mark."

Jimmy hid his face behind a book.

...continued next page

1. READING:LITERATURE

"Is that true?" asked Ms. Jones. Claire and Abby nodded. Ms. Jones asked Jimmy to stand up. She told him he would have to go to the principal's office and explain what he had done.

Jimmy began to cry. "I'm sorry, Ms. Jones. I really am."

Ms. Jones pointed toward the classroom door. "Hurry along now, Jimmy," said Ms. Jones. Jimmy left the room and went to the principal's office. "Now let's get back to writing in our notebooks," said Ms. Jones. The students nodded their heads and began to write in their notebooks once more.

=== TRUE OR FALSE ===

5. The setting is a fifth-grade classroom. (RL.2.7)

   A. True   **B.** False

6. The plot of the story is that you should do your work right the first time. (RL.2.7)

   A. True   **B.** False

7. There are eight characters in the story. (RL.2.7)

   A. True   **B.** False

8. The illustration shows where each student sits in the classroom. (RL.2.7)

   A. True   **B.** False

1. READING: LITERATURE

> **Directions:** *Read the poem and answer the questions below.*

LUNCHTIME

I love when it is lunchtime.
I get to open my lunch bag
And see all the food that's mine.
My favorite food to eat is pizza

With lots of melted cheese.
The food I hate the most
Would have to be green peas!
I always drink ice-cold milk

To wash my food down.
I like to add chocolate sauce,
Which makes the milk turn brown.
Sitting at the lunch table is fun,

My friends are all so silly.
We all eat together,
Sandy, Ashley, me, and Billy.
Every day at noon,

We gather in the cafeteria.
All in all, I have to say,
Lunchtime Is my favorite time of day!

1. READING: LITERATURE

=== MULTIPLE CHOICE ===

9. **What is this poem about?** (RL.2.4)
    - **A.** Meeting friends
    - **B.** Going to school
    - **C.** Cleaning the cafeteria
    - **D.** Eating lunch

10. **Which of these words or phrases from the poem is descriptive?** (RL.2.4)
    - **A.** Open
    - **B.** Eat
    - **C.** Melted cheese
    - **D.** Drink

11. **Which of these words or phrases from the poem is descriptive?** (RL.2.4)
    - **A.** Green peas
    - **B.** Friends
    - **C.** Cafeteria
    - **D.** Day

12. **Which of these words in the poem rhymes with *cheese*?** (RL.2.4)
    - **A.** Mine
    - **B.** Brown
    - **C.** Silly
    - **D.** Peas

> **Directions:** *Read the passage and answer the questions below.*

THE GOOSE THAT LAID THE GOLDEN EGGS

There once was a man who owned a wonderful goose. Every morning, the goose laid for him a big, beautiful egg — an egg made of pure, shiny, solid gold. Every morning, the man collected golden eggs. And little by little, egg by egg, he began to grow rich. But the man wanted more.

"My goose has all those golden eggs inside her," he kept thinking. "Why not get them all at once?"

One day he couldn't wait any longer. He grabbed the goose and killed her. But there were no eggs inside her!

"Why did I do that?" the man cried. "Now there will be no more golden eggs."

1. READING: LITERATURE

=== FREE RESPONSE ===

13. What is the central message of the story? (RL.2.2)

_____

_____

_____

_____

_____

_____

=== MULTIPLE CHOICE ===

14. What did the man want? (RL.2.2)

- **A.** He wanted to have another goose.
- **B.** He wanted to have lots of eggs.
- **C.** He wanted to be rich.
- **D.** He wanted to have beautiful things.

15. What lesson could the man have learned in this story? (RL.2.2)

- **A.** Take care of your animals.
- **B.** Appreciate what you have.
- **C.** Try to get more of what you have.
- **D.** Work hard and you will succeed.

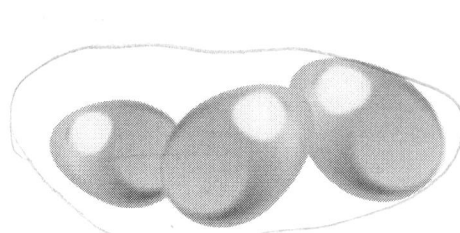

1. READING: LITERATURE

> **Directions:** *Read the passage and answer the questions below.*

HELPING OUR PLANET

The students in Ms. Smith's second-grade class wanted to celebrate Earth Day. They decided they would split up into two teams to work on a class project. Ms. Smith asked for two volunteers to be team captains.

"I will lead one of the teams," said Taylor.

"And I will lead the other team," said Josie.

Ms. Smith thanked Taylor and Josie for raising their hands to volunteer. She asked the two students to come up to her desk and pick up instructions for the project. Taylor was joined by 15 other students while the other 14 remaining students joined Josie's team. Each team met on opposite sides of the classroom and got busy working.

"What should we do for our project?" Taylor asked his group. "Does anyone have any good ideas?" The students sat in silence for a few minutes thinking. "I think we should do our project on recycling," said Taylor. "We use so much paper in the classroom," he explained. "We need to help save the trees by recycling the paper we use daily." The other team members quickly agreed. "Ms. Smith!" Taylor exclaimed. "Our team has chosen to take up recycling for our project."

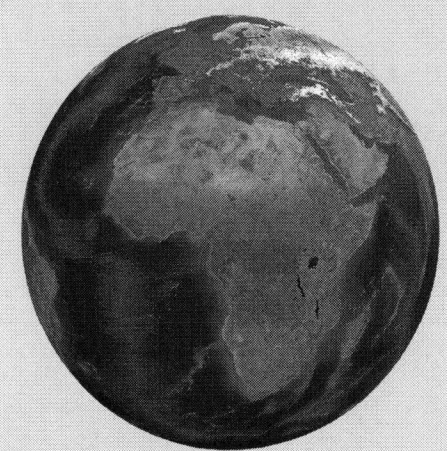

Meanwhile, the other team was still thinking about what they wanted to do. All of a sudden, Josie called out, "I've got it! We should make our playground more beautiful. We could plant flowers and trees." Josie's teammates liked her idea. Ms. Smith liked the plan, too.

Now both teams had decided on their class projects. The students got right to work recycling paper and planting trees and flowers. Together, they were helping our planet!

1. READING: LITERATURE

FREE RESPONSE

16. Who speaks in the story? How do you know? (RL.2.6)

_____
_____
_____
_____
_____
_____
_____
_____

17. Who is telling the story? How do you know? (RL.2.6)

_____
_____
_____
_____
_____
_____
_____
_____

1. READING:LITERATURE

18. How do you think the students felt about doing a class project to celebrate Earth Day? (RL.2.6)

_____
_____
_____
_____
_____
_____
_____

19. Why do you think Taylor and Josie volunteered as team captains? (RL.2.6)

_____
_____
_____
_____
_____
_____
_____
_____

1.4. CHAPTER REVIEW

1. READING: LITERATURE

> **Directions:** *Read the passages and answer the questions below.*

THE TORTOISE AND THE HARE

One spring day, Hare was hopping through a field. Duck, Cow, Pig, and Tortoise were enjoying the sun together.

"You know," said Hare. "I have never been beaten in a race. Not once has anyone – or anything – run faster than me. Would any of you like to challenge me?"

The other animals looked at each other, none of them eager to lose a race to Hare, for Hare would never stop bragging about it. At last, Tortoise said, "I will race you, Hare. I accept your challenge."

"You are too funny, Tortoise," said Hare. "I could pass the finish line five times before you even start the race. Seriously, you'll be eating my dust!"

"I'll ask you to keep your bragging to yourself until the race is done," said Tortoise.

"It won't be long then. Shall we race?" asked Hare. Tortoise just nodded his head – slowly.

The other animals decided on a course. "Okay, line up," said Pig. "On your mark, get set, go!" Hare was halfway down the dusty lane before Tortoise even had his legs over the starting line.

"Slow and steady," said Tortoise. "Slow and steady."

By this time, Hare was almost to the bridge. He looked back to see if he could spot Tortoise. He wasn't sure if it was Tortoise, but there was a green and brown lump moving toward him very slowly. "My goodness," thought Hare, "I could take a nap and still win this race. Wait! I could take a nap and win." Hare curled up on the ground and, laughing to himself, fell asleep.

As Tortoise inched his way forward, Hare dreamed of running past the finish line, shaking hands with the other animals, and eating carrots. As he woke from his dream, Hare rubbed his eyes and saw Tortoise – crossing the finish line. "No!" shouted Hare. "I'm faster!"

"Slow and steady wins the race, Hare," said Tortoise with a smile. "Slow and steady."

1. READING: LITERATURE

The Town Mouse And The Country Mouse

A Town Mouse once visited a relative who lived in the country. For lunch, the Country Mouse served wheat stalks, roots, and acorns, with a dash of cold water to drink. The Town Mouse ate very sparingly, nibbling a little of this and a little of that. She was eating the simple food just to be polite.

After the meal, the friends had a long talk. The Town Mouse talked about her life in the city while the Country Mouse listened. They then went to bed in a cozy nest in the barn and slept in quiet and comfort until morning. In her sleep, the Country Mouse dreamed she was a Town Mouse. She dreamed of all the luxuries and delights of city life that her friend had described. The next day when the Town Mouse asked the Country Mouse to go home with her to the city, she gladly said yes.

When they reached the mansion in which the Town Mouse lived, they found on the table in the dining room the remains of a very fine meal. There were sweetmeats and jellies, pastries, and delicious cheeses. Just as the Country Mouse was about to nibble a dainty bit of pastry, she heard a Cat meow loudly and scratch at the door. In great fear the Mice scurried to a hiding place. They lay quite still for a long time, hardly daring to breathe. When they thought it was clear, they went back to the table. When they were about to eat, the door opened suddenly and a massive dog came in.

That night, the Country Mouse grabbed her belongings. "You may have luxuries that I do not have," she said to the Town Mouse as she hurried away, "but I prefer my plain food and simple life in the country with the peace and security that go with it."

1. READING:LITERATURE

TRUE OR FALSE

20. Both stories include animals as the main characters. (RL.2.9)

    A. True   **B.** False

21. Both stories center around a race between the main characters. (RL.2.9)

    A. True   **B.** False

22. The ending of both stories is similar. (RL.2.9)

    A. True   **B.** False

23. Both stories involved someone winning. (RL.2.9)

    A. True   **B.** False

> **Directions:** *Read the passage and answer the questions below.*

Valentine's Day

    Jackie is so excited because today is Valentine's Day. Her school allows the students to celebrate this holiday. She spent a lot of time making homemade Valentine's cards. Her dad and her also spent time making little goody bags with toys, candy, yo-yos, and silly putty. She closed the bags with a pretty red ribbon. Her dad drove her to school and helped her carry in her cards and gifts.

    As Jackie walked into her classroom, she was so surprised. Her teacher, Mrs. Catchem, decorated the entire classroom with red streamers, hearts, and red balloons. It looked so nice.

    After the morning bell and morning math work, it was time for their party. The teacher told the students to get out their Valentine's Day cards and get ready to pass them out. Jackie was getting her box out that she created to gather all of her cards. She looked beside her and saw Ezra with his head down. She shrugged and thought that he never paid attention to what the teacher said. Ezra just sat there with his head down on the desk. The teacher then announced that she will be calling out table numbers to pass out cards.

    "Tables one and two, please" said Mrs. Catchem.

1. READING: LITERATURE

> Jackie leaned over to Ezra. "Get out your cards, Ezra," she said to him. Ezra lifted his head, looked at her, and then sadly looked down at his feet. Oh, thought Jackie. She finally realized that Ezra didn't have any Valentine's cards.
>
> "Tables three and four, please" announced Mrs. Catchem.
>
> Table three is Jackie and Ezra's table. Jackie turned around quickly and put the box of gifts on Ezra's desk. She was happy that she didn't put her name on them. She said in a loud voice so all her classmates would hear, "Wow Ezra! These goody bags you made are great!"
>
> Ezra was confused at first, but then he caught on. Ezra quickly got up out of his seat and passed out the goody backs to his classmates.
>
> Later that day, she received a handwritten letter on red paper on her desk. She opened it up. It said, "Thanks for being a friend. Happy Valentine's Day. Love, Ezra."

MULTIPLE CHOICE

24. Why does Jackie give her goody bags to Ezra? (RL.2.3)
- **A.** He gave her gifts the previous day.
- **B.** They were originally his gifts.
- **C.** He helped her make the gifts.
- **D.** Jackie felt bad because Ezra didn't have anything to give away for Valentine's Day.

FILL IN THE BLANK

25. Jackie was surprised when she walked into the classroom and saw _____. (RL.2.3)

TRUE OR FALSE

26. If Jackie hadn't given Ezra her goody bags, Ezra wouldn't have anything to give away to the class. (RL.2.3)

- **A.** True
- **B.** False

1. READING: LITERATURE

> **Directions:** *Read the passage and answer the questions below.*

MOVING DAY

On Saturday afternoon, Julia spotted the moving truck outside of her bedroom window. It was finally moving day.

Julia let out a sigh. She looked around her room at her toys spread out on the floor. Julia grabbed an empty box and began packing up her toys.

"Are you almost ready to go?" called her mom.

Julia moved quickly to grab the rest of her toys. "Yes!" she said.

When everything in her room was gone, Julia stood in the middle of the floor. She looked around at the walls and windows. She just stood there quietly remembering all the fun times she had in her room. She felt a tear on her cheek.

Julia walked over to the light switch and turned off the lights for the last time. She closed the door and headed out of her old house. Her mom was outside with the moving truck.

"Let's hurry and get to the new house before it gets too dark," said her mom.

Julia got in the car and drove with her mom over to their new house.

"Here it is!" said her mom. "Julia, you are going to love it here. I know you loved your old room, but your new room is much bigger."

Julia slowly walked into the new house. Her mom pointed to the door of her new room. As Julia opened the door, a big smile came across her face. Her mom was right. This room was much bigger than her old one. It had more windows, too. The walls were painted bright pink. This was her favorite color. Julia would feel right at home here.

1. READING:LITERATURE

=== MULTIPLE CHOICE ===

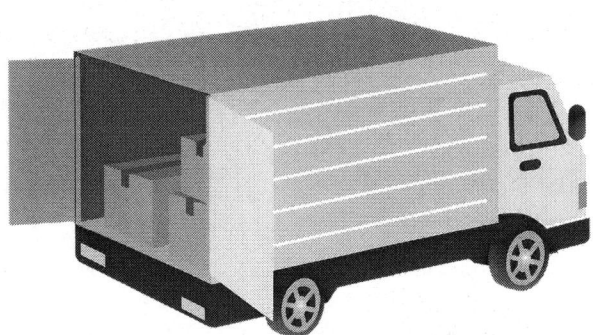

27. What is this story about? (RL.2.5)
- A. A moving truck
- B. Packing up an old bedroom
- C. Moving to a new house
- D. Julia and her mom

28. Who is Julia? (RL.2.5)
- A. A neighbor
- B. A friend
- C. The main character of the story
- D. The mom

29. What does the beginning of the story tell you? (RL.2.5)
- A. The setting
- B. That it is moving day
- C. Information about the main character
- D. What Julia's room looks like

30. Where does the story take place? (RL.2.5)
- A. On a Saturday afternoon
- B. At Julia's old house then at her new house
- C. In Julia's bedroom
- D. Inside a moving truck

1.4. CHAPTER REVIEW

2. READING: INFORMATIONAL TEXT

2.1. KEY IDEAS AND DETAILS — 56
- Text details
- Main idea
- Sequence

2.2. CRAFT AND STRUCTURE — 64
- Understanding vocabulary
- Locate information
- Author's point of view

2.3. INTEGRATION OF KNOWLEDGE AND IDEAS — 73
- Visual illustrations
- Text connections
- Compare/contrast key details

2.4. CHAPTER REVIEW — 86

2. READING: INFORMATIONAL TEXT

2.1. Key Ideas and Details

Common Core State Standards: CCSS.ELA-LITERACY.RI.2.1, CCSS.ELA-LITERACY.RI.2.2, CCSS.ELA-LITERACY.RI.2.3

Skills:
- Demonstrate an understanding of key details in a text
- Identify the main topic
- Describe the connection between a series of historical events, scientific ideas or concepts, or steps in technical procedures in a text

> **Directions:** *Read the passage and answer the questions below.*

ORANGES

1 Oranges are round, juicy fruits that grow on trees in places with warm weather. How does an orange get from the tree to your refrigerator?

2 People who work as fruit pickers move through groves filled with orange trees. When an orange is ripe, the picker clips it off the tree. All picked oranges are then carefully moved to a packing plant.

3 In the plant, oranges are placed on a machine with moving rollers. Special brushes wash the fruit as it rolls along. Next, each orange is dried.

4 Another machine lines up the oranges in boxes. A computer checks each box. Any oranges with spots or damage are removed. Orange growers want to produce good fruit that people will buy.

5 Finally, each orange is given a sticker and placed in a box. Full boxes are shipped in cool trucks to stores.

...continued next page

2. READING: INFORMATIONAL TEXT

6 People who work in the store place the oranges on shelves. Then someone from your family comes to the store. Your family member chooses a few oranges, buys them, brings them home, and puts them in your refrigerator.

7 Then, one day, you open your refrigerator—and there those oranges are, ready for you to eat!

FREE RESPONSE

---

1. **What is the main topic of this article?** (RI.2.2)

   _____

   _____

   _____

   _____

   _____

   _____

2. **How are oranges checked?** (RI.2.1)

   _____

   _____

   _____

   _____

   _____

   _____

   _____

2.1. KEY IDEAS AND DETAILS

2. READING: INFORMATIONAL TEXT

FILL IN THE BLANK

3. **Where are oranges cleaned and packaged?**
   _____ (RI.2.1)

4. **Where do oranges grow?**
   Oranges grow in places with _____ weather. (RI.2.1)

5. **Who removes oranges from trees?**
   The _____ removes oranges from the trees. (RI.2.1)

TRUE OR FALSE

6. **When oranges arrive at the packing plant they are put on a machine with moving rollers.** (RI.2.3)
   A. True B. False

7. **Paragraph six is about how oranges move from stores to people's homes.** (RI.2.2)
   A. True B. False

8. **The next step after picking the orange is drying it.** (RI.2.3)
   A. True B. False

2.1. KEY IDEAS AND DETAILS

> **Directions:** Read the passage and answer the questions below.

Twisting Tornadoes

1 At around eight o' clock at night on October 12, 2015, the skies were getting very dark in Nappanee, Indiana. In this small Amish town there is a resort with a theatre. On the evening of October 12, many people were watching a musical at the theatre. At around nine o'clock, the local Nappanne storm siren went off, shocking citizens. People all over the town of Nappanee got in their basements.

...continued next page

2. READING: INFORMATIONAL TEXT

The people at the theater went into the bathrooms. A tornado was headed towards downtown Nappanne. Moments later it hit exactly where meteorologists said it would. This devastating tornado hit the Burger King, destroyed the grocery store, and demolished Kentucky Fried Chicken. Businesses and homes were destroyed. Five people died in this tragic storm.

2 After this tornado passed, many people of this little town checked on their neighbors and loved ones to see if they were safe and not injured. Cell phones were not working after the storm and many people were panicking. Citizens were worried about their loved ones.

How Tornadoes Form

3 The definition of the word tornado is a natural disaster that consists of a destructive vortex of winds that turn in a circle at a very fast rate. Tornadoes don't just come out of nowhere, there are certain factors that make a tornado appear. The perfect environment for a tornado is similar to the environment in a thunderstorm. Tornadoes occur when hot air mixes with the cold air. This meeting of two different air temperatures makes the wind move in a whirlwind direction.

4 Tornadoes do not occur everywhere around the world. Certain places are more likely to have tornadoes. They usually are spotted in the Midwestern states of the United States. When thinking of tornadoes, many people think of the state of Kansas due to the tornado that took the main character Dorothy in the movie The Wizard of Oz. Kansas is a state that is part of tornado alley, which is a group of states that have the most tornadoes. These states in tornado alley are Texas, Olkhamoma, Kansas, Nebraska, South Dakota, Missouri, Illinois, Indiana, and Ohio. Every year there are more than five hundred tornadoes that occur within the states in tornado alley.

Do We Know When A Tornado Is Coming?

5 Scientists who view and study the weather and natural disasters are called meteorologists. Meteorologists use a lot of technological equipment in order to predict upcoming tornadoes. With their equipment, they can see how many miles a tornado is away from a certain area and how fast the tornado is going. With this information, they can predict when a tornado is going to hit a particular location.

2. READING: INFORMATIONAL TEXT

Because tornadoes don't move super fast like hurricanes, it is easier for meteorologists to see where a tornado is headed. The meteorologists then give warnings on the radio, the Internet, and television in order to warn the public about a dangerous tornado in an area. When meteorologists give their warnings, they say there is either a tornado watch or a tornado warning. A tornado watch tells people that the environment is ideal for a tornado to occur. A tornado warning tells the public that a tornado has been spotted in the area. A tornado warning is more dangerous than a tornado watch.

6 Meteorologists were heroes when it came to the people of Nappanee, Indiana in 2015. The messages and warnings from the meteorologists on the television, radio, and Internet helped save lives. They warned people to get inside their homes. They warned the spectators at the theater to stop the show and seek shelter. They saved lives with their warnings

2.1. KEY IDEAS AND DETAILS

=== FREE RESPONSE ===

9. Why do so many tornadoes happen in Kansas? (RI.2.1)

_____

_____

_____

10. How are thunderstorms and tornadoes related? (RI.2.3)

_____

_____

_____

11. What is the main idea of this text? (RI.2.2)

_____

_____

2. READING: INFORMATIONAL TEXT

_____

_____

=== TRUE OR FALSE ===

12. Tools that meteorologists use tell them how fast a tornado is moving. (RI.2.1)

  A. True   **B.** False

13. Tornadoes move very fast which makes it hard to tell where they will go and how long it will take. (RI.2.1)

  A. True   **B.** False

=== MULTIPLE CHOICE ===

14. What does a tornado "warning" mean? (RI.2.1)

  A. A tornado warning means that a tornado touched down.
  B. A tornado warning means that a tornado already happened.
  C. A tornado warning means that a tornado could happen.
  D. A tornado warning means that a tornado could be dangerous.

15. Why did the author add the story about the tornado that occurred in Nappanee, Indiana? (RI.2.2)

  A. To grab the audience's attention about a dangerous tornado
  B. To show the audience that tornadoes can be avoided
  C. To tell the audience a story to entertain them
  D. To help the audience understand difficult vocabulary words

16. What is the main idea of paragraph six? (RI.2.2)

  A. Meteorologists can predict where and when tornadoes will occur.
  B. Tornadoes are extremely dangerous natural disasters.
  C. Basements keep citizens safe.
  D. Meteorologists help save people's lives with their warnings.

2.1. KEY IDEAS AND DETAILS

2. READING: INFORMATIONAL TEXT

> **Directions:** *Read the passage and answer the questions below.*

The History of the Hula Hoop

1 Have you ever played with a hula hoop? Can you keep the hula hoop up as you shake your hips? The hula hoop has been around since the mid-1900s. Two friends named Arthur Melin and Richard Knerr invented it. They were owners and creators of the company Wham-O. They made many toys in the 1900s. Their most famous toys were the hula hoop, the boomerang, and the frisbee.

2 The two owners of this company decided to make the hula hoop in 1948 when they were inspired by seeing children in other countries play with wooden hoops. They would often dance with them. Arthur Melin and Richard Knerr wanted to make a lightweight plastic hula hoop instead so kids would not get hurt and it wouldn't be too heavy for them. The creators called their new invention a hula hoop based off of hula dancing. Hula dancers from Hawaii often move their hips in a certain manner. This is the same movement needed in order to keep a hula hoop up, spinning, and off the ground.

3 The hula hoop was very popular when it first came out, but it didn't last too long like other toys. However, hula hoops are still sold today and many children own one. Some people even use the hula hoop to break records. In 2004, a winning record was achieved. A person held up a hula hoop for one hundred revelations. How long can you keep a hula hoop up?

2.1. KEY IDEAS AND DETAILS

FREE RESPONSE

17. How did the creators of the hula hoop come up with the idea for this new toy? (RI.2.3)

_____
_____
_____
_____

NAME: _____ DATE: _____

2. READING: INFORMATIONAL TEXT

18. How did the creators come up with the name hula hoop? (RI.2.3)

_____
_____
_____
_____
_____

19. What is the main idea of paragraph three? (RI.2.1)

_____
_____
_____
_____
_____

— TRUE OR FALSE —

20. Arthur Melin and Richard Knerr created the company Wham-O.

(RI.2.3)

A. True **B.** False

2.1. KEY IDEAS AND DETAILS

2.2. CRAFT AND STRUCTURE

2. READING: INFORMATIONAL TEXT

2.2. Craft and Structure

Common Core State Standards: CCSS.ELA-LITERACY.RI.2.4, CCSS.ELA-LITERACY.RI.2.6

Skills:
- Determine the meaning of words and phrases in a text
- Identify the main purpose of a text, including what the author wants to answer, explain, or describe

> **Directions:** Read the articles and answer the questions below.

ARTICLE 1

So much traffic is zipping around Earth's orbit. An orbit is the path of one space object around another. Scientists have to keep an eye on all that traffic to make sure it flows smoothly.

People have sent hundreds of satellites into Earth's orbit. A satellite is an object that orbits a planet. Some travel as close as 100 miles above Earth. Others are thousands of miles away. The satellites have different jobs. Some track the weather. Other satellites send signals to radios, televisions, cell phones, and computers.

The Hubble Space Telescope is a well-known satellite. It was launched into space in 1990. It is in orbit 380 miles above Earth. Hubble takes photos of our solar system and faraway galaxies. A galaxy is a huge group of stars, dust, and gas. Over the years, Hubble has taught scientists a lot about space.

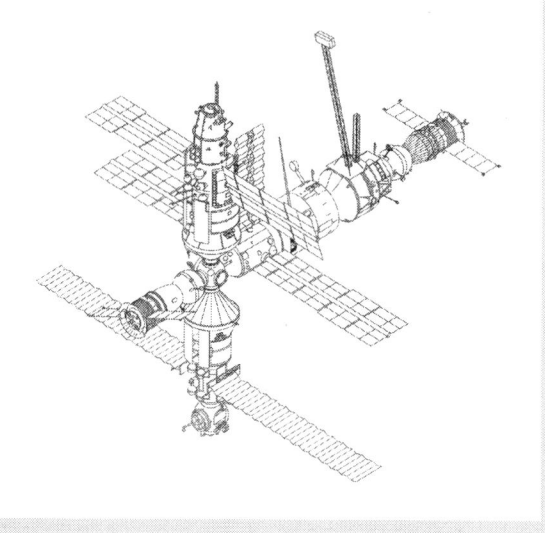

The International Space Station is a special type of satellite. It is a giant research lab in space where astronauts live and work. The station is in orbit 220 miles above Earth. Work on the space station began in 1998. It was finished in 2011. It is about the size of a five-bedroom house.

2. READING: INFORMATIONAL TEXT

ARTICLE 2

When you look into the sky, what do you see? The sun, the moon, the stars, and clouds, right? What about trash? Believe it or not, there is trash, otherwise known as space debris, flying around the Earth very far away. It is so far away that your eyes can't see it.

How in the word did trash get there? This debris is not like the trash you are thinking of that litter our parks and beaches. Space debris consists of old broken pieces of existing satellites in our solar system. There are very small pieces of debris and extremely large pieces as well. The bigger pieces of debris are larger than people. This debris broke off of satellites and rockets.

Is this debris a problem? Space debris is a problem in the solar system just like trash is on Earth. Debris in the solar system is dangerous because it could hit existing satellites. The debris could cause damage to them, make them not work, and even create more debris.

Scientists do a great job of watching this debris to make sure it isn't collecting more and is staying away from existing satellites. The job is not an easy one though. There are a lot of satellites and a lot of fast moving debris. Many scientists all over the world, not just in the United States, are trying to solve this dilemma. Hopefully soon there will be an answer.

=== FREE RESPONSE ===

1. **What is a satellite?** (RI.2.4)

_____

_____

_____

_____

_____

2. READING: INFORMATIONAL TEXT

2. **What does the term orbit mean?** (RI.2.4)

_____
_____
_____
_____

=== FILL IN THE BLANK ===

3. **The junk in space is called** _____. (RI.2.4)

4. **The International Space Station is a unique type of** _____. (RI.2.4)

=== MULTIPLE CHOICE ===

5. **What is the main purpose of Article 1?** (RI.2.6)
   A. The main purpose is to teach readers about the Hubble Space Telescope.
   B. The main purpose is to teach readers about the International Space Station.
   C. The main purpose is to teach readers about satellites and the important work they do.
   D. The main purpose is to teach readers about space trash and how it can harm satellites.

6. **What is the main purpose of Article 2?** (RI.2.6)
   A. The main purpose is to teach readers about satellites and the important work they do.
   B. The main purpose is to teach readers about space debris and the possible problems it can cause.
   C. The main purpose is to explain how satellites break off in space.
   D. The main purpose is to teach readers about NASA and the word they do.

2.2. CRAFT AND STRUCTURE

2. READING: INFORMATIONAL TEXT

> **Directions:** *Read the article and answer the questions below.*

President Spotlight: Grover Cleveland

Stephen Grover Cleveland was born in 1837 in New Jersey. When he was young, he enjoyed school. However, tragedy struck his life. Cleveland's father died when he was an adolescent. This caused him to quit school. He got a job to support his mother and siblings.

Cleveland helped out in many law offices. This work inspired him to study to become a lawyer. After being a lawyer for a couple of years, he became the sheriff of his town. He wanted to get into politics. He ran for mayor and won. As mayor, he was known for saving money and helping out citizens. After being mayor, he wanted something bigger and better. Cleveland became the governor of New York. In 1884, he then ran for president. He became the Democratic nominee. He then won against Republican Blaine. The vote was close. Cleveland was voted as president. He won by just a thousand votes. As president of the United States, Cleveland was most famous and popular for helping gain back Native American land.

After his first four years as president, Cleveland ran for reelection in 1888. However, due to the increase of taxes when he was president, he was not well liked. He lost the election to Benjamin Harrison. However, he did not stop there. What is unique about President Cleveland is that he was the 22nd President of the United States and also the 24th President of the United States. Four years later, he ran again and won. He was determined to finish what he started. President Cleveland died in 1908.

2.2. CRAFT AND STRUCTURE

―――――― **FREE RESPONSE** ――――――

7. **What happened during Grover Cleveland's childhood?** (RI.2.4)

_____

_____

_____

2. READING: INFORMATIONAL TEXT

8. **The author wants to give the article another title that conveys the main purpose of the passage. What title should the author use for this passage? Explain.** (RI.2.6)

_____

_____

_____

_____

_____

_____

=== MULTIPLE CHOICE ===

9. **What is the author trying to explain in this text?** (RI.2.6)
    A. Who a diplomat is
    B. Interesting facts about President Grover Cleveland
    C. How Grover Cleveland lost the election
    D. Why Grover Cleveland liked politics

10. **Why did Grover Cleveland drop out of school?** (RI.2.4)
    A. He did not enjoy school.
    B. He was not a strong student.
    C. His family moved too much.
    D. He had to get a job to support his family.

=== FILL IN THE BLANK ===

11. Grover Cleveland was the _____ and _____ president of the United States. (RI.2.4)

12. President Grover Cleveland was most famous for _____
_____ (RI.2.4)

2.2. CRAFT AND STRUCTURE

2. READING: INFORMATIONAL TEXT

> **Directions:** *Read the articles and answer the questions below.*

CANAIMA NATIONAL PARK

In 1962, the Venezuelan government created Canaima National Park. A national park is an area of land that is protected from people who want to cut down its trees or hunt the animals living in it. The Venezuelan government wanted to make sure that this land was protected because it has many beautiful features. These features include mountains called *tepuis* that are known for their flat tops. Canaima National Park also has cliffs and waterfalls.

Some animals that live in the park are endangered. This means that these animals are in danger of going extinct. There are five endangered animal species that live in this park. One of these species is the jaguar.

=== FREE RESPONSE ===

13. What is a national park? (RI.2.4)

_____
_____
_____
_____
_____
_____
_____

2. READING: INFORMATIONAL TEXT

14. What is the main purpose of this text? (RI.2.6)

_____

_____

_____

_____

_____

_____

_____

_____

_____

15. Why do you think the author wanted to describe Canaima National Park? (RI.2.6)

_____

_____

_____

_____

_____

_____

_____

_____

_____

2.2. CRAFT AND STRUCTURE

2. READING: INFORMATIONAL TEXT

16. What is a tepuis? (RI.2.4)

_____

_____

_____

_____

17. What does it mean for an animal to be endangered? (RI.2.4)

_____

_____

_____

_____

> **Directions:** Read the article and answer the questions below.

The Rocky Mountains

The Appalachian Mountains is the oldest mountain range on Earth. Scientists know this due to the type of rocks that make up the mountains. They also know this due to the way the mountains are formed and how they eroded over time. The Appalachian Mountains stretch across the northeastern part of North America. The mountains reside mostly in the United States, but the range does cross the Canadian border. The mountain range is almost two thousand miles long. The highest peak of the Appalachian Mountains is six thousand feet high. Scientists believe that the Appalachian Mountains were taller than the Rocky Mountains or the Alps.

...continued next page

2. READING: INFORMATIONAL TEXT

> However, due to erosion, the Appalachian Mountains are not as high.
> In the past, the Appalachian Mountains were home to many Native Americans. They settled near the mountain for protection. The mountains were also an excellent source of water and food. The Appalachian Mountains provide many water sources in the form of springs, waterfalls, and rivers. There are also many animals in this area including bear, bison, wolves, and elk. Even moose live in the northern regions of the Appalachian Mountains. Today, people walk the Appalachian Trail and go to the national parks in the area.

=== MULTIPLE CHOICE ===

2.2. CRAFT AND STRUCTURE

18. What is the author describing in this text? (RI.2.6)
   A. How big mountains are
   B. What people like to do in the mountains
   C. The Appalachian Mountains
   D. The Alps

19. What countries do the Appalachian Mountains touch? (RI.2.4)
   A. The United States and Canada
   B. North America and Canada
   C. The United States and Europe
   D. France and North America

20. What can a tourist do when visiting the Appalachian Mountains? (RI.2.4)
   A. They can visit the Rocky Mountains.
   B. They can hike the Appalachian Trail.
   C. They can swim in the ocean.
   D. They can visit California.

2.3. INTEGRATION OF KNOWLEDGE AND IDEAS

2. READING: INFORMATIONAL TEXT

2.3. Integration of Knowledge and Ideas

Common Core State Standards: CCSS.ELA-LITERACY.RI.2.8, CCSS.ELA-LITERACY.RI.2.9

Skills:
- Describe how reasons support specific points the author makes in a text
- Compare and contrast the most important points presented by two texts on the same topic

> **Directions:** Read the articles and answer the questions below.

Article 1

So much traffic is zipping around Earth's orbit. An orbit is the path of one space object around another. Scientists have to keep an eye on all that traffic to make sure it flows smoothly.

People have sent hundreds of satellites into Earth's orbit. A satellite is an object that orbits a planet. Some travel as close as 100 miles above Earth. Others are thousands of miles away. The satellites have different jobs. Some track the weather. Others send signals to radios, televisions, cell phones, and computers.

The Hubble Space Telescope is a well-known satellite. It was launched into space in 1990. It is in orbit 380 miles above Earth. Hubble takes photos of our solar system and faraway galaxies. A galaxy is a huge group of stars, dust, and gas. Over the years, Hubble has taught scientists a lot about space.

The International Space Station is a special type of satellite. It is a giant research lab in space where astronauts live and work. The station is in orbit 220 miles above Earth. Work on the space station began in 1998. It was finished in 2011. It is about the size of a five-bedroom house.

Article 2

When you look into the sky, what do you see? The sun, the moon, the stars, and clouds, right? What about trash? Believe it or not, there is trash, otherwise known as space debris, flying around the Earth very far away. It is so far away that your eyes can't see it.

...continued next page

2. READING: INFORMATIONAL TEXT

How in the word did trash get there? This debris is not like the trash you are thinking of that litter our parks and beaches. Space debris consists of old broken pieces of existing satellites in our solar system. There are very small pieces of debris and extremely large pieces as well. The bigger pieces of debris are larger than people. This debris broke off of satellites and rockets.

Is this debris a problem? Space debris is a problem in the solar system just like trash is on Earth. Debris in the solar system is dangerous because it could hit existing satellites. The debris could cause damage to them, make them not work, and even create more debris.

Scientists do a great job of watching this debris to make sure it isn't collecting more and is staying away from existing satellites. The job is not an easy one though. There are a lot of satellites and a lot of fast moving debris. Many scientists all over the world, not just in the United States, are trying to solve this dilemma. Hopefully soon there will be an answer.

FREE RESPONSE

1. **How are Articles 1 and 2 different?** (RI.2.9)

2. READING: INFORMATIONAL TEXT

2. **Articles 1 and 2 both talk about satellites. How do they talk about satellites differently?** (RI.2.9)

_____

_____

_____

_____

_____

_____

_____

3. **How does the author of Article 2 support the claim that space junk is a problem?** (RI.2.8)

_____

_____

_____

_____

_____

_____

_____

2.3. INTEGRATION OF KNOWLEDGE AND IDEAS

2. READING: INFORMATIONAL TEXT

TRUE OR FALSE

4. If a reader wanted to learn about different types of satellites it would be better for them to read Article 1 than Article 2. (RI.2.9)

A. True **B.** False

> **Directions:** *Read the article and answer the questions below.*

President Spotlight: Grover Cleveland

Stephen Grover Cleveland was born in 1837 in New Jersey. When he was young, he enjoyed school. However, tragedy struck his life. Cleveland's father died when he was an adolescent. This caused him to quit school. He got a job to support his mother and siblings.

Cleveland helped out in many law offices. This work inspired him to study to become a lawyer. After being a lawyer for a couple of years, he became the sheriff of his town. He wanted to get into politics. He ran for mayor and won. As mayor, he was known for saving money and helping out citizens. After being mayor, he wanted something bigger and better. Cleveland became the governor of New York. In 1884, he then ran for president. He became the Democratic nominee. He then won against Republican Blaine. The vote was close. Cleveland was voted as president. He won by just a thousand votes. As president of the United States, Cleveland was most famous and popular for helping gain back Native American land.

After his first four years as president, Cleveland ran for reelection in 1888. However, due to the increase of taxes when he was president, he was not well liked. He lost the election to Benjamin Harrison. However, he did not stop there. What is unique about President Cleveland is that he was the 22nd President of the United States and also the 24th President of the United States. Four years later, he ran again and won. He was determined to finish what he started. President Cleveland died in 1908.

2. READING: INFORMATIONAL TEXT

FREE RESPONSE

5. How does the author support the point that President Grover Cleveland was a unique president? (RI.2.8)

_____
_____
_____
_____
_____
_____

> **Directions:** *Read the article and answer the questions below.*

ARTICLE 1 ANIMALS OF AFRICA

Africa is home to some of the most majestic animals on Earth. Let's take a close look at some of these animals.

AFRICAN ELEPHANTS

African elephants are the largest animals on Earth that live on land. They travel in groups called herds. These herds are usually made up of related female elephants and their calves. Males normally travel by themselves. But sometimes they also form small groups with other males.

Like all elephants, African elephants have very long noses called trunks. They suck in water through their trunks and spray it over their bodies. This helps them stay cool in the heat. They also breathe and grab things with their trunks.

...continued next page

2.3. INTEGRATION OF KNOWLEDGE AND IDEAS

African elephants eat roots, grasses, fruit, and tree bark. They can eat up to 300 pounds of food in a day!

Giraffes

Giraffes are beautiful spotted animals. They have very long necks. They're also the tallest animals to walk the earth. Giraffes live in areas covered by grass. These areas are called grasslands.

Giraffes have great vision. With the help of their height and vision, they can easily spot predators, such as lions, from a distance. It's believed that other animals such as zebras form groups near giraffes for this reason! They know if danger is coming, giraffes will see it.

Lions

Everyone knows lions are the kings of the jungle, right? Well, they don't actually live in jungles! They live in grasslands, just like giraffes. They also live in deserts.

Lions form groups called prides. Anywhere from 3 to 40 lions may live in one pride. Female lions (called lionesses) raise the cubs and hunt for food. They hunt mainly at night in small groups. Male lions defend the area where the pride is staying. They use their loud roars to scare off other animals trying to get too close.

Article 2   African Animals

Much of the continent of Africa is a savanna. A savanna is an open grassland with few trees. Africa's savanna is home to many different types of animals.

The savanna is a habitat. A habitat is a place where an animal lives. Here are some animals that live in the African savanna.

Lion

Lions are big cats with gold-colored fur. Lions are carnivores (KARneh-vawrz). Carnivores are meat eaters. Lions live together in a group called a **pride**.

...continued next page

2. READING: INFORMATIONAL TEXT

ELEPHANT

Elephants are animals with trunks and tusks. Elephants are herbivores (ER-beh-vawrz). Herbivores are plant eaters. Elephants live together in a group called a **herd**.

GIRAFFE

Giraffes are the tallest animals in the world. They are plant eaters. Their height helps them reach leaves on tall trees. Giraffes live in a herd of about 10 animals.

WARTHOG

Warthogs are a type of wild hog. Warthogs are omnivores (AHM-nehvawrz). Omnivores eat both plants and meat. Female and baby warthogs live in a small group called a **sounder**. Males live alone.

HIPPOPOTAMUS

Hippopotamuses are animals that live partly on land and partly in the water. They are herbivores that eat mainly grasses. Hippos live in a herd of up to 15 members.

FREE RESPONSE

6. **Compare where the two articles say giraffes live.** (RI.2.9)

_____
_____
_____
_____

2.3. INTEGRATION OF KNOWLEDGE AND IDEAS

2. READING: INFORMATIONAL TEXT

2.3. INTEGRATION OF KNOWLEDGE AND IDEAS

7. **What is one important point that is made in both articles?** (RI.2.9)

8. **What is one important point that is in Article 2 but not in Article 1?** (RI.2.9)

9. **How does the author of Article 1 support the opinion, "Giraffes are beautiful"?** (RI.2.8)

2. READING: INFORMATIONAL TEXT

FILL IN THE BLANK

10. If a reader wants to learn about how giraffes stay safe from predators they should read Article _____. (RI.2.9)

TRUE OR FALSE

11. If a reader wanted to learn about many different animals in Africa, Article 1 would be better for them to read than Article 2. (RI.2.9)

   A. True
   B. False

> **Directions:** *Read the articles and answer the questions below.*

ARTICLE 1   THE POWER OF THE EARTH

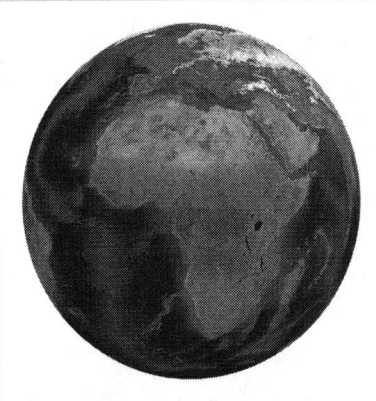

Imagine you are walking into your kitchen to get a snack when all of a sudden the ground is shaking, cups are rattling in the sink, and cans are falling off shelves. What in the world is happening? The definition of an earthquake is a natural disaster that occurs when the ground shakes. This motion starts deep within the Earth. Earthquakes cause a lot of damage. This damage can be done to roads and buildings. It also causes huge waves to hit the shore as earthquakes are more popular on the coast.

How do earthquakes form? Our Earth is made up of four different layers. The top layer, the one that we can see with our eyes, is called the crust. Under the crust, where we can't see is the mantle, then the outer core, and then the inner core. While we may think that the earth is one solid ball, it really isn't. It has many tectonic plates. Think of these plates as large pieces of rocks. The plates are always moving above the core of the Earth. They usually move slowly, which means we don't feel it.

...continued next page

However, when the tectonic plates hit each other, we can feel it and it causes damage to the Earth. This makes the other layers collide and this causes pressure to build up. If a little pressure is released then the Earth shakes just a little bit. But if a lot of pressure is released then the Earth shakes a lot. This can cause a lot of damage.

Article 2 Why Are There Earthquakes?

In the year 1960, the largest earthquake in the world hit Valdivia, Chile in South America. This was a 9.5 magnitude earthquake. The higher the number, the worse the earthquake. Thousands of buildings were destroyed. Millions of people lost their homes. Citizens of Valdivia were not safe after the earthquake. There were many aftershocks. This means that there were more little earthquakes afterwards. This made the rubble and destruction shift and create more damage. This earthquake also caused a tsunami or a giant wave to hit the shore. The earthquake and tsunami caused more than six thousand deaths.

Earthquakes are natural disasters that happen very quickly. It is hard to one hundred percent tell when they are coming and where they will hit. Earthquakes happen very frequently, however, they are not too big and don't create much damage. Sometimes people don't even feel the smaller earthquakes. However, the stronger the earthquake the more damage it causes. Earthquakes are caused when the rough and jagged tectonic plates hit each other and pull away from each other. When they pull away, this releases pressure. The more pressure that is released the more damage it causes.

2. READING: INFORMATIONAL TEXT

FREE RESPONSE

12. What is one main point both articles are making? (RI.2.9)

_____

_____

_____

_____

13. What is one main point that is in Article 2 but not in Article 1? (RI.2.9)

_____

_____

_____

_____

14. What is one main point that is in Article 1 but not in Article 2? (RI.2.9)

_____

_____

_____

_____

2. READING: INFORMATIONAL TEXT

MULTIPLE CHOICE

15. Earthquakes happen very _____ and it is hard to tell when and where they will occur. (RI.2.8)

    A. quickly
    B. slowly
    C. oddly
    D. quietly

16. If a reader wanted to learn about tectonic plates, which article should they read? (RI.2.9)

    A. Article 1
    B. Article 2
    C. Neither Article 1 or 2
    D. The dictionary

17. What is the best evidence the author of Article 2 gives to support the statement, "earthquakes are not rare"? (RI.2.8)

    A. Most earthquakes are weak and many people don't know they happen.
    B. Earthquakes happen quickly.
    C. Earthquakes are caused by tectonic plates.
    D. Earthquakes are dangerous.

FILL IN THE BLANK

18. If a reader wants to read a real story about an earthquake, then they should read Article _____. (RI.2.9)

> **Directions:** Read the article and answer the questions below.

Appalachian Mountains

The Appalachian Mountains is the oldest mountain range on Earth. Scientists know this due to the type of rocks that make up the mountains. They also know this due to the way the mountains are formed and how they eroded over time.

...continued next page

2. READING: INFORMATIONAL TEXT

The Appalachian Mountains stretch across the northeastern part of North America. The mountains reside mostly in the United States, but the range does cross the Canadian border. The mountain range is almost two thousand miles long. The highest peak of the Appalachian Mountains is six thousand feet high. Scientists believe that the Appalachian Mountains were taller than the Rocky Mountains or the Alps. However, due to erosion, the Appalachian Mountains are not as high.

In the past, the Appalachian Mountains were home to many Native Americans. They settled near the mountain for protection. The mountains were also an excellent source of water and food. The Appalachian Mountains provide many water sources in the form of springs, waterfalls, and rivers. There are also many animals in this area including bear, bison, wolves, and elk. Even moose live in the northern regions of the Appalachian Mountains. Today, people walk the Appalachian Trail and go to the national parks in the area.

2.3. INTEGRATION OF KNOWLEDGE AND IDEAS

=== MULTIPLE CHOICE ===

19. What information does the author give to support the point, "The Appalachian Mountains are the oldest mountain range on Earth"? (RI.2.8)

   A. "Scientists know this due to the type of rocks that make up the mountains."
   B. "The mountains were also an excellent source of water and food."
   C. "However, due to erosion, the Appalachian Mountains are not as high."
   D. "The Appalachian Mountains stretch across the northeastern part of North America."

=== TRUE OR FALSE ===

20. The purpose of this text is to teach us about all mountains. (RI.2.8)

   A. True   **B.** False

2.4. CHAPTER REVIEW

2. READING: INFORMATIONAL TEXT

2.4. Chapter Review

> **Directions:** *Read the passage and answer the questions below.*

Twisting Tornadoes

1 At around eight o' clock at night on October 12, 2015, the skies were getting very dark in Nappanee, Indiana. In this small Amish town there is a resort with a theatre. On the evening of October 12, many people were watching a musical at the theatre. At around nine o'clock, the local Nappanne storm siren went off, shocking citizens. People all over the town of Nappanee got in their basements. The people at the theater went into the bathrooms. A tornado was headed towards downtown Nappanne. Moments later it hit exactly where meteorologists said it would. This devastating tornado hit the Burger King, destroyed the grocery store, and demolished Kentucky Fried Chicken. Businesses and homes were destroyed. Five people died in this tragic storm.

2 After this tornado passed, many people of this little town checked on their neighbors and loved ones to see if they were safe and not injured. Cell phones were not working after the storm and many people were panicking. Citizens were worried about their loved ones.

How Tornadoes Form

3 The definition of the word tornado is a natural disaster that consists of a destructive vortex of winds that turn in a circle at a very fast rate. Tornadoes don't just come out of nowhere, there are certain factors that make a tornado appear. The perfect environment for a tornado is similar to the environment in a thunderstorm. Tornadoes occur when hot air mixes with the cold air. This meeting of two different air temperatures makes the wind move in a whirlwind direction.

4 Tornadoes do not occur everywhere around the world. Certain places are more likely to have tornadoes. They usually are spotted in the Midwestern states of the United States.

...continued next page

2. READING: INFORMATIONAL TEXT

When thinking of tornadoes, many people think of the state of Kansas due to the tornado that took the main character Dorothy in the movie The Wizard of Oz. Kansas is a state that is part of tornado alley, which is a group of states that have the most tornadoes. These states in tornado alley are Texas, Olkhamoma, Kansas, Nebraska, South Dakota, Missouri, Illinois, Indiana, and Ohio. Every year there are more than five hundred tornadoes that occur within the states in tornado alley.

Do We Know When A Tornado Is Coming?

5 Scientists who view and study the weather and natural disasters are called meteorologists. Meteorologists use a lot of technological equipment in order to predict upcoming tornadoes. With their equipment, they can see how many miles a tornado is away from a certain area and how fast the tornado is going. With this information, they can predict when a tornado is going to hit a particular location. Because tornadoes don't move super fast like hurricanes, it is easier for meteorologists to see where a tornado is headed. The meteorologists then give warnings on the radio, the Internet, and television in order to warn the public about a dangerous tornado in an area. When meteorologists give their warnings, they say there is either a tornado watch or a tornado warning. A tornado watch tells people that the environment is ideal for a tornado to occur. A tornado warning tells the public that a tornado has been spotted in the area. A tornado warning is more dangerous than a tornado watch.

6 Meteorologists were heroes when it came to the people of Nappanee, Indiana in 2015. The messages and warnings from the meteorologists on the television, radio, and Internet helped save lives. They warned people to get inside their homes. They warned the spectators at the theater to stop the show and seek shelter. They saved lives with their warnings.

2. READING: INFORMATIONAL TEXT

=== FREE RESPONSE ===

1. **How is a tornado watch related to a tornado warning?** (RI.2.3)

   _____
   _____
   _____
   _____
   _____

2. **Your teacher tells you to ask your friend a question about the article that starts with the word "when." What question do you ask your friend?** (RI.2.1)

   _____
   _____
   _____
   _____
   _____
   _____

2. READING: INFORMATIONAL TEXT

3. **How do tornadoes begin?** (RI.2.3)

   _____

   _____

   _____

4. **What is the main idea of paragraph three?** (RI.2.2)

   _____

   _____

   _____

FILL IN THE BLANK

5. Paragraph _____ tells about the tornado alley. (RI.2.2)

6. Paragraph _____ tells how tornadoes are tracked and how the public is warned about them. (RI.2.2)

7. Why do people think of the state of Kansas when referring to tornadoes? (RI.2.1)

   _____

   _____

2. READING: INFORMATIONAL TEXT

8. Who uses radar to track tornadoes and other storms? _____ (RI.2.1)

9. How many states are part of "tornado alley"? _____

   _____ (RI.2.1)

=== TRUE OR FALSE ===

10. **Radar can tell us how fast a tornado is moving.** (RI.2.1)

    A. True   **B.** False

11. **Tornados move very fast so it is hard to tell where they will go and when they will hit.** (RI.2.1)

    A. True   **B.** False

=== MULTIPLE CHOICE ===

12. **Which paragraph explains a real tornado that was dangerous to a small town?** (RI.2.2)

    A. Paragraph 1   **B.** Paragraph 2
    C. Paragraph 3   **D.** Paragraph 4

> **Directions:** Read the article and answer the questions below.

THE FIRST AMERICAN WOMAN DOCTOR

Elizabeth Blackwell was the first woman to become a medical doctor in the United States. Elizabeth was born in England more than a hundred years ago. She moved to the U.S. when she was about eleven years old.

At first, Elizabeth was a teacher. Later, she knew she wanted to study medicine.

Elizabeth applied to many medical schools in the United States, but they would not take her. These schools were only allowing men to study medicine. Finally, Elizabeth found a school that let her in.

...continued next page

2. READING: INFORMATIONAL TEXT

> Some men at the school did not want a woman there. At first, they were not kind to her.
>
> After two years, Elizabeth graduated at the top of her class at the medical school. She and her sister opened a clinic for women and children in New York City. They gave medical care to the poor. Dr. Blackwell also opened a medical college for women. She trained women to become doctors. She also gave speeches and wrote books.
>
> Dr. Elizabeth Blackwell had courage and a strong character. She worked hard for the things she wanted to do. Her work encouraged other women to become doctors.

FREE RESPONSE

13. What is the purpose of this text? (RI.2.6)

_____
_____
_____
_____
_____

14. What reasons does the author give to support the claim "Dr. Elizabeth Blackwell had courage and strong character"? (RI.2.8)

_____
_____
_____
_____
_____

2.4. CHAPTER REVIEW

2. READING: INFORMATIONAL TEXT

15. What do you think the author wants us to learn from this article? (RI.2.6)

_____
_____
_____
_____
_____

16. What reasons does the author give to support the claim "Her work encouraged other women to become doctors"? (RI.2.8)

_____
_____
_____
_____
_____

=== MULTIPLE CHOICE ===

17. Which reason best supports the author's claim that Elizabeth Blackwell "worked hard for the things she wanted to do"? (RI.2.8)

A. She wanted to study medicine and be a doctor.
B. She opened a clinic with her sister.
C. She applied to medical schools even though they were only accepting men.
D. She opened a medical school in New York City.

2. READING: INFORMATIONAL TEXT

> **Directions:** *Read the article and answer the questions below.*

THE THREE BRANCHES OF GOVERNMENT

The United States Constitution was written over two hundred years ago. It explains how the United States government should work. The people who wrote the Constitution did not want one person or a group to have too much power. That was why they divided the government into three parts, known as branches.

The branches are the legislative, the executive, and the judicial. Each branch has its own responsibilities. The branches work together, but they also check each other to make sure no branch has too much power.

The legislative branch includes the United States Congress. Congress is made up of the House of Representatives and the Senate. Voters in each state elect their representation in the House and their senators. Those men and women go to Washington, D.C., to make laws.

The executive branch has the power to carry out laws. It includes the president, the vice president, and their group of advisers called the Cabinet. Every four years, Americans vote to elect a president and a vice president.

The judicial branch decides on the meanings of the laws and whether laws break the rules of the Constitution. This branch includes the United States Supreme Court. Nine justices serve on the Supreme Court. The president appoints the justices, and the Senate approves them. The justices' job is to decide if the country's laws go against the Constitution.

2. READING: INFORMATIONAL TEXT

=== FREE RESPONSE ===

18. What is the author of this text explaining? (RI.2.6)

_____

_____

_____

_____

19. What does the phrase "branches of government" mean? (RI.2.4)

_____

_____

_____

_____

_____

=== MULTIPLE CHOICE ===

20. In this context, the word "branches" means _____ (RI.2.4)
  - **A.** A piece of a tree
  - **B.** Congress
  - **C.** Parts
  - **D.** Government

21. The main purpose of this text is to teach the reader about _____ (RI.2.6)
  - **A.** how the United States Supreme Court works.
  - **B.** the legislative branch.
  - **C.** the United States Constitution.
  - **D.** how power is divided among the three branches.

2. READING: INFORMATIONAL TEXT

FILL IN THE BLANK

22. In this article, the term _____ is referring to people who serve on the Supreme Court. (RI.2.4)

TRUE OR FALSE

23. In this article, the term "Cabinet" is referring to a group of advisers. (RI.2.4)

   A. True **B.** False

> **Directions:** *Read the articles and answer the questions below.*

ARTICLE 1 IN MEMORY OF DR. KING

A piece of the nation's capital will honor an important leader—Dr. Martin Luther King Jr. A memorial for King is being built on the National Mall in Washington, D.C. It will be the first memorial on the Mall to honor an African American.

A ceremony was held on November 13, [2006] to mark the start of construction. President George W. Bush and other leaders were among the thousands of people who gathered for the event.

"When the work is done, the King memorial will be a fitting tribute—powerful and hopeful and poetic—like the man it honors," Bush said at the ceremony.

ARTICLE 2 HONORING A GREAT AMERICAN

Dr. King is honored with a **memorial**. A memorial is a statue or a place that honors a person or an event. The King Memorial is built on the National Mall. That is a park in Washington, D.C., our nation's capital. Memorials for some U.S. presidents are also on the Mall.

...continued next page

2. READING: INFORMATIONAL TEXT

> The King Memorial opened in August of 2011. It has a 30-foot statue of King. Sentences from some of his speeches are carved into a stone wall.
>
> The cost of the memorial was $100 million. A concert was held in September 2010 in New York City to raise some of the money. Many famous singers performed. The singers included Aretha Franklin, Stevie Wonder, and Garth Brooks.

=== FREE RESPONSE ===

24. How are these two articles related? (RI.2.9)

_____
_____
_____
_____
_____
_____
_____

25. What does the author of Article 1 want to explain to readers? (RI.2.6)

_____
_____
_____
_____
_____
_____
_____

2. READING: INFORMATIONAL TEXT

26. **Compare how the two articles describe the King memorial.** (RI.2.9)

_____
_____
_____
_____

27. **Compare and contrast the ceremony and concert discussed in the articles.** (RI.2.9)

_____
_____
_____
_____

28. **What is a memorial?** (RI.2.4)

_____
_____
_____
_____

2. READING: INFORMATIONAL TEXT

29. **What is the purpose of Article 2?** (RI.2.6)

   _____
   _____
   _____
   _____
   _____

30. **What point do you think the author of Article 2 was trying to make with the sentence, "Memorials for some U.S. presidents are also on the Mall"?** (RI.2.9)

   _____
   _____
   _____
   _____
   _____

3. READING: FOUNDATIONAL SKILLS

3.1. PHONICS AND WORD RECOGNITION   100
- ❖ Distinguish long and short vowels
- ❖ Decode regularly spelled two-syllable words with long vowels
- ❖ Decode words with common prefixes and suffixes

3.2. CHAPTER REVIEW   107

3. READING: FOUNDATIONAL SKILLS

3.1. Phonics and Word Recognition

Common Core State Standard: CCSS.ELA-LITERACY.RF.2.3

Skills:

- Know and apply grade-level phonics and word analysis skills in decoding words.
- Distinguish long and short vowels when reading regularly spelled one-syllable words.
- Know spelling-sound correspondences for additional common vowel teams.
- Decode regularly spelled two-syllable words with long vowels.
- Decode words with common prefixes and suffixes.
- Identify words with inconsistent but common spelling-sound correspondences.
- Recognize and read grade-appropriate irregularly spelled words.

=== EXAMPLE QUESTIONS ===

> **Directions:** *Read the sentences below. Identify whether the underlined word has a short or long vowel sound.*

E1 The children would <u>spin</u> very fast on the merry-go-round.

    A. Short vowel   **B.** Long vowel

Answer: **A.** The word *spin* has a short vowel sound. The "i" vowel does not make an "i" sound.

E2 Which of these words has a long vowel sound? (RF.2.3.A)

    A. ship   **B.** shape   **C.** shock   **D.** shell

Answer: **B.** The word *shape* has the long /a/ sound.

3. READING: FOUNDATIONAL SKILLS

E3 **Which of these words has a long /e/ vowel blend?** (RF.2.3.B)

   A. paint   **B.** coach   **C.** beam   **D.** house

Answer: **C.** The word *beam* has a long /e/ vowel blend. The vowel blend *ea* makes the long /e/ sound.

E4 **Which word best completes the sentence?** (RF.2.3.D)

I _____ lemons because they are too sour.

   A. likely   **B.** dislike   **C.** liked   **D.** likeness

Answer: **B.** The prefix *dis-* means "not" or "opposite." The subject expresses that lemons are too sour. The word *dislike* best completes this sentence.

E5 **Which of these words has the same *gh* as the underlined word?** (RF.2.3.E)

Alligators have <u>rough</u> skin.

   A. ghost   **B.** sight   **C.** dough   **D.** tough

Answer: **D.** The consonant blend *gh* can make different sounds. In the words *rough* and *tough* the letters *gh* make the /f/ sound.

E6 **Which of these words has an irregular spelling?** (RF.2.3.F)

   A. funny   **B.** silly   **C.** busy   **D.** gloomy

Answer: **C.** The word *busy* has an irregular spelling. Irregularly spelled words have letters that make an unusual sound. In the word *busy*, the letter u makes the short /i/ sound and the letter s makes the /z/ sound.

3.1. PHONICS AND WORD RECOGNITION

3. READING: FOUNDATIONAL SKILLS

Common Core State Standard: CCSS.ELA-LITERACY.RF.2.4

Skills:
- Read with sufficient accuracy and fluency to support comprehension.
- Read grade-level text with purpose and understanding.
- Read grade-level text orally with accuracy, appropriate rate, and expression on successive readings.
- Use context to confirm or self-correct word recognition and understanding, rereading as necessary.

3.1. PHONICS AND WORD RECOGNITION

=== EXAMPLE QUESTION ===

➤ **Directions:** *Mark the following statements as either true or false.*

E1 Readers should read at a slow and steady pace.

  A. True   **B.** False

Answer: **A.** The reader should not read too fast but at a slow and steady pace.

➤ **Directions:** *Read the passage. Then answer the questions that follow.*

TRIP TO THE MUSEUM

Ava's second grade class had been learning about different places around the <u>globe</u>. Her teacher, Mr. Adams, told the class that they were going on a field trip. He was taking the students to the museum.

=== MULTIPLE CHOICE ===

➤ **Directions:** *Choose the best answer.*

1. **Does the underlined word globe have a short or long vowel sound?** (RF.2.3)

   A. Short vowel   **B.** Long vowel

3. READING: FOUNDATIONAL SKILLS

2. **Why were the students going to the museum?** (RF.2.4)
   A. Because they wanted to
   B. Because their teacher took them on a field trip there
   C. Because they had already been to the zoo
   D. Because the museum was close to the school

> The students were looking forward to seeing the things they had learned about up close. Ava and her classmates were very excited. They wondered what they would see. The bus driver found a place to park. The students ran inside the museum.

3. **Say the word bus. Does the word have a short or long vowel sound?** (RF.2.3)

   A. Short vowel
   B. Long vowel

4. **Which word has a short a vowel sound?** (RF.2.3)
   A. place
   B. park
   C. a
   D. Ava

5. **What should you do if you don't know what the word wondered means?** (RF.2.4)
   A. You should ignore it and keep reading
   B. You should ask the teacher
   C. You should guess what the word means
   D. You should use a dictionary to look up the meaning of the word

3.1. PHONICS AND WORD RECOGNITION

3. READING: FOUNDATIONAL SKILLS

> Inside the museum, each student was given a card. On the card there was a special <u>code</u> number. The student would use this number during their trip. It would tell them more information about the different items in the museum.

6. **Does the underlined word <u>code</u> have a short or long vowel sound?** (RF.2.3)

    A. Short vowel **B.** Long vowel

7. **Why was each student given a card?** (RF.2.4)
    A. Because it was their ticket to get into the museum
    B. Because it was a pass
    C. Because it had a code on it that they would use
    D. Because it had money on it

8. **What did the code number do?** (RF.2.4)
    A. It unlocked doors
    B. It got the students into the museum
    C. It told the students a secret message
    D. It gave the students more information about items in the museum

> Ava and her classmates walked around the museum. One room was closed off with a rope. Ava <u>tried</u> to take a look inside. Mr. Adams was behind her. He cleared his <u>throat</u>. "Ava, we should not be looking in there," said Mr. Adams. Ava agreed. "I'm sorry, Mr. Adams. I was just curious."

9. **What is the vowel team for the word <u>tried</u> that makes a long vowel sound?** (RF.2.3)

    A. tr **B.** ri **C.** ie **D.** ed

10. **What is the vowel team for the word <u>throat</u> that makes a long vowel sound?** (RF.2.3)

    A. th **B.** ro **C.** oa **D.** at

3.1. PHONICS AND WORD RECOGNITION

3. READING: FOUNDATIONAL SKILLS

> **Directions:** *Read the song. Then answer the questions that follow.*

TAKE ME OUT TO THE BALL GAME

Take me out to the ball game,
Take me out with the crowd.

TRUE OR FALSE

> **Directions:** *Mark the following statements as either true or false.*

11. **These song lyrics are sung at a baseball game.** (RF.2.4)

    A. True **B.** False

12. **The song is asking a question.** (RF.2.4)

    A. True **B.** False

> Buy me some <u>peanuts</u> and crackerjack, I
> don't care if I never get back.

13. **The vowel team for the word <u>peanuts</u> that makes a long vowel sound is: ea** (RF.2.3)

    A. True **B.** False

14. **The song lyrics are asking for something.** (RF.2.4)

    A. True **B.** False

15. **If you don't know what crackerjack is, you should guess.** (RF.2.4)

    A. True **B.** False

3.1. PHONICS AND WORD RECOGNITION

3. READING: FOUNDATIONAL SKILLS

> Let me <u>root, root,</u> root for the home <u>team</u>,
> If they don't win, it's a shame.

16. **The word <u>root</u> means to cheer.** (RF.2.4)

    A. True   **B.** False

17. **The vowel team for the word <u>team</u> that makes a long vowel sound is: te** (RF.2.3)

    A. True   **B.** False

> For it's one, two, three <u>strikes</u>, you're out,
> At the old ball game.

18. **The ball player gets three strikes before they're out of the game.** (RF.2.4)

    A. True   **B.** False

19. **The word <u>strikes</u> means to swing a bat really fast.** (RF.2.4)

    A. True   **B.** False

20. **You should pause when reading the line: "one, two, three."** (RF.2.4)

    A. True   **B.** False

3.1. PHONICS AND WORD RECOGNITION

3.2. CHAPTER REVIEW

3. READING: FOUNDATIONAL SKILLS

3.2. Chapter Review

> **Directions:** Read the question and select the best answer choice.

=== MULTIPLE CHOICE ===

1. **Which of these words has a short vowel sound?** (RF.2.3.A)
   - **A.** chase
   - **B.** blast
   - **C.** trail
   - **D.** dream

2. **Which of these words has a long vowel sound?** (RF.2.3.A)
   - **A.** flip
   - **B.** sock
   - **C.** time
   - **D.** bread

3. **Which of these two-syllable words has a long vowel sound?** (RF.2.3.C)
   - **A.** rainy
   - **B.** thinner
   - **C.** candle
   - **D.** bucket

4. **Which of these words has a long /o/ vowel blend?** (RF.2.3.B)
   - **A.** crooked
   - **B.** throat
   - **C.** pocket
   - **D.** soiled

5. **Which of these words has the same /s/ sound as the underlined word?** (RF.2.3.E)

   I like to <u>visit</u> my grandmother.
   - **A.** summer
   - **B.** bossy
   - **C.** sound
   - **D.** desert

6. **Which of these words has an irregular spelling?** (RF.2.3.F)
   - **A.** creamy
   - **B.** people
   - **C.** spoon
   - **D.** thump

7. **Which word best completes the sentence?** (RF.2.3.D)

   Be _____ while walking on the ice.
   - **A.** careful
   - **B.** careless
   - **C.** caring
   - **D.** care

3. READING: FOUNDATIONAL SKILLS

> **Directions:** *Circle the correct word in each sentence.*

8. Read the sentence. Circle the word with an irregular spelling. (RF.2.3.F)

We are going to see the play again on Sunday.

9. Read the sentences. Circle the two words that have the same /ow/ sound. (RF.2.3.E)

The show is about a wise owl and his friends. We are sitting in the first row.

10. Read the sentence. Circle the word with a prefix that means "not." (RF.2.3.D)

The fox was very unkind. The owl teaches him about kindness.

> **Directions:** *Read the poem. Then answer the questions that follow.*

DADDY FELL INTO THE POND

Everyone grumbled. The sky was grey.
We had nothing to do and nothing to say.
We were nearing the end of a dismal day,

=== FILL-IN-THE-BLANK ===

> **Directions:** *Write the correct answer on the blank line.*

11. The poem has many two-syllable words with long vowels. Read the first line of the poem. Write a two-syllable word you read _____ (RF.2.3)

3. READING: FOUNDATIONAL SKILLS

> And there seemed to be nothing beyond,
> THEN
> *Daddy fell into the pond!*

12. **The poem has many two-syllable words with long vowels. Read the first line of the poem. Write a two-syllable word you read** _____ (RF.2.3)

> And everyone's face grew merry and bright,
> And Timothy danced for sheer delight.
> "Give me the camera, quick, oh quick!
> He's crawling out of the duckweed." Click!

13. **Look at the picture. Fix the spelling of the word below.** (RF.2.3)

ermaac

_____

14. _____ **was crawling out of the duckweed.** (RF.2.4)

15. **Another word for crawling is** _____ . (RF.2.4)

3.2. CHAPTER REVIEW

3. READING: FOUNDATIONAL SKILLS

> Then the gardener suddenly slapped his knee,
> And doubled up, shaking silently,
> And the ducks all quacked as if they were daft,
> And it sounded as if the old drake laughed.

16. **Read the word shaking in the second line. Draw a line between the letters below to break the word up into two syllables.** (RF.2.3)

sha|king

17. **Read the word sounded in the fourth line. Draw a line between the letters below to break the word up into two syllables.** (RF.2.3)

sounded

18. **The ducks made a _____ sound.** (RF.2.4)

> O, there wasn't a thing that didn't respond,
> WHEN
> *Daddy fell into the pond!*

19. **Read the word respond in the first line. Draw a line between the letters below to break the word up into two syllables.** (RF.2.3)

respond

20. **The word _____ is in all capital letters to tell the reader to shout the word.** (RF.2.4)

3. READING: FOUNDATIONAL SKILLS

> **Directions:** *Read the passage. Then answer the questions that follow.*

GRIZZLY BEARS

Brown bears are also known as grizzly bears. Their fur comes in many shades of color. Some are light brown. Other bears are dark brown. They can reach up to eight feet tall when they stand on their hind legs. They weigh hundreds of pounds. A large female can weigh up to 800 pounds. They are quite fast and can move quickly. They can run up to 30 miles an hour.

— FREE RESPONSE —

21. Look at the picture. Fix the spelling of the word below. (RF.2.3)

lyzgrzi

_____

Use the word in a sentence.

_____

_____

_____

3. READING: FOUNDATIONAL SKILLS

22. Do you think it is surprising that grizzly bears are fast? Why or why not? (RF.2.4)

_____

_____

_____

> Grizzly bears use sounds and smells to talk to each other. They also scratch their bodies on trees to let other bears know they are nearby. The other bears will <u>decode</u> the body language. Grizzlies live in North America. They can be found in forests and meadows. They can also be seen in woodlands and prairies. Some live in Yellowstone National Park. Many live along rivers and streams. They eat many different things. The bears enjoy the <u>goodness</u> of sweet berries, fruit, roots, leaves, nuts, insects, birds, and fish. Grizzly bears also hunt for rodents, sheep, elk, and moose.

23. Does the word <u>decode</u> have a prefix, suffix, or both? Use the word in a sentence. (RF.2.3)

_____

_____

_____

24. Does the word <u>goodness</u> have a prefix, suffix, or both? Use the word in a sentence. (RF.2.3)

_____

_____

_____

3. READING: FOUNDATIONAL SKILLS

25. Where do grizzly bears live? (RF.2.4)

_____

_____

_____

26. How do grizzly bears talk to each other? (RF.2.4)

_____

_____

_____

> Starting in the fall season, grizzly bears go into a <u>deep</u> <u>sleep</u> called hibernation. They hibernate for five to <u>eight</u> months. The bears dig dens into a hillside. Inside, they sleep all day and <u>night</u>. They hide from the <u>snow</u> and female bears <u>give</u> birth to cubs.

27. Read the word pairs <u>deep</u> and <u>sleep</u>. What are other words that are spelled like them but said differently? (RF.2.3)

_____

_____

_____

28. Read the word pairs <u>eight</u> and <u>night</u>. What are other words that are spelled like them but said differently? (RF.2.3)

_____

_____

_____

3.2. CHAPTER REVIEW

3. READING: FOUNDATIONAL SKILLS

29. Read the word <u>give</u> in the last sentence of the passage. What are some words that are spelled like it? (RF.2.3)

_____

_____

_____

30. What is hibernation? Use the details in the text to help you. (RF.2.4)

_____

_____

_____

4. WRITING

4.1. TEXT TYPES AND PURPOSES   **116**
- Opinion pieces
- Informative/explanatory writing
- Narrative writing

4.2. CHAPTER REVIEW   **127**

4. WRITING

4.1. Text Types and Purposes

Common Core State Standards: CCSS.ELA-LITERACY.W.2.1, CCSS.ELA-LITERACY.W.2.2, CCSS.ELA-LITERACY.W.2.3

Skills:

- Write opinion pieces in which they introduce the topic or book they are writing about, state an opinion, supply reasons that support the opinion, use linking words (e.g., because, and, also) to connect opinion and reason, and provide a concluding statement or section.
- Write informative/explanatory texts in which they introduce a topic, use facts and definitions to develop points, and provide a concluding statement or section.
- Write narratives in which they recount a well-elaborated event or short sequence of events, include details to describe actions, thoughts, and feelings, use temporal words to signal event order, and provide a sense of closure.

=== EXAMPLE ===

> **Directions:** *Read the passage and answer the questions below.*

Kids should only eat healthy snacks. Junk food does not have enough vitamins. Candy is too sweet and can hurt your teeth. Also, healthy snacks are fresher than junk food. A ripe, crisp apple is better than a soggy, packaged snack cake. In fact, kids should never eat unhealthy snacks.

E1 **What is the author's opinion in this text?** (W.2.1)

    A. Kids should eat both junk food and healthy snacks.
    B. Kids should only eat healthy snacks.
    C. Kids should brush their teeth every day.
    D. Kids should take vitamins.

Answer: **B.** The author's opinion is that kids should only eat healthy snacks.

4. WRITING

EXAMPLE

> The Pacific Ocean covers 30% of the Earth. It also provides more than half of the Earth's water. The Pacific Ocean is the deepest ocean on Earth, too. It is over 12,000 feet deep! The deepest point of the Pacific Ocean, called Challenger Deep, is the lowest part of the Earth's crust. All of these features make the Pacific Ocean the largest body of water on Earth.

E2 **Which sentence best introduces the topic?** (W.2.2)

- **A.** The ocean was named by an explorer, Ferdinand Magellan back in 1521.
- **B.** The Pacific Ocean covers 30% of the Earth.
- **C.** All of these features make the Pacific Ocean the largest body of water on Earth.
- **D.** The name Pacific means "peaceful" in Latin.

Answer: **C.** The sentence "The Pacific Ocean covers 30% of the Earth" best introduces the topic of this text.

EXAMPLE

DAISY DAWSON IS ON HER WAY

> The butterfly was still for a few moments. Then, very slowly, it spread its wings and fluttered gracefully up into the air. Daisy shielded her eyes against the sun and blinked as the butterfly swooped low past her face, brushing her cheek gently with the tip of its wing. Then it rose once more into the warm air and flew high into the treetops, growing smaller and smaller until finally it was lost from sight. As Daisy watched it fly away, her cheek began to tingle as though something was sparkling beneath her skin. She touched a hand to her face, and a delicious warm feeling fizzed along her fingers, tumbling like a wave through her whole body until it reached all the way down to the tips of her toes.

4.1. TEXT TYPES AND PURPOSES

4. WRITING

E3 **Which sentence best describes the character's actions and feelings?** (W.2.3)

- **A.** She touched a hand to her face, and a delicious warm feeling fizzed along her fingers, tumbling like a wave through her whole body until it reached all the way down to the tips of her toes.
- **B.** Then it rose once more into the warm air and flew high into the treetops, growing smaller and smaller until finally it was lost from sight.
- **C.** The butterfly was still for a few moments.
- **D.** Daisy shielded her eyes against the sun and blinked as the butterfly swooped low past her face, brushing her cheek gently with the tip of its wing.

Answer: **A.** This sentence best describes the character's actions and feelings.

4.1. TEXT TYPES AND PURPOSES

4. WRITING

> **Directions:** *Read the passage and answer the questions below.*

Gender Neutral Toy Aisles?

Imagine you are at Walmart and your grandparents say that you can go to the toy aisle to pick out a toy. You are ecstatic! You go to the toy aisle! What do you see? Usually, the toy aisles are separated by age. You see a baby aisle first. You avoid that aisle as you are not a baby. How are the other toy aisles organized? Well, typically, there are boy toy aisle and girl toy aisles. But should there be? Are some toys for boys and some for girls? Or can anyone play with any toy they want?

Many people think that by having a girl aisle and a boy aisle that it helps people find what they are looking for. Many people think that having separate toy aisle by gender keeps the store and toys organized. For example, the cars are together, the dolls are together, and the legos are together. But can a boy get a doll and a girl get a superhero toy? Of course! Boys and girls should be able to play with whatever toy they want to play with.

MULTIPLE CHOICE

1. **What is the author's opinion in this text?** (W.2.1)
   A. Stores should not separate toys by gender.
   B. Stores should separate toys by gender.
   C. Girls should not buy superhero toys.
   D. Boys should buy cars.

2. **Which sentence best supports the author's opinion?** (W.2.1)
   A. Many stores put toys aimed at boys in one place.
   B. They put toys aimed at girls in another.
   C. It makes the store more organized.
   D. Some kids like this.

3. **Which sentence uses a linking word to connect opinion and reasons?** (W.2.1)
   A. Say you're looking for a doll
   B. For kids, it's easier to find what they are looking
   C. Who cares if the aisles are separated by gender?
   D. A girl can look for a doll and then cars.

4. WRITING

> **Directions:** Read the passage and answer the questions below.

Goodbye, Bake Sales?

Bake sales are popular. They help schools raise money. Families bake sweet treats. Students sell the treats. The school earns money. It is used to help pay for field trips. It is also used to pay for art and sports programs.

Some people think it is good to limit the sale of sweet treats. They say that will reduce health problems among kids. Others say the rules make it harder for schools to raise money.

I think sweets should be banned from school because they aren't good for children. Some schools have bake sales to raise money. But there are other ways to do that. For example, schools can have raffles or sell water. Schools should care more about students' health than they do about fundraising.

=== MULTIPLE CHOICE ===

4. **Which sentence best describes the author's opinion in this text?** (W.2.1)
   A. I think sweets should be banned from school because they aren't good for children.
   B. Some people think it is good to limit the sale of sweet treats.
   C. Others say the rules make it harder for schools to raise money.
   D. Some schools have bake sales to raise money.

5. **Which sentence does not support the author's opinion in this text?** (W.2.1)
   A. Schools should care more about students' health than they do about fundraising.
   B. For example, schools can have raffles or sell water.
   C. Bake sales are popular.
   D. They say that will reduce health problems among kids.

4. WRITING

6. Which underlined word acts as a linking word? (W.2.1)

<u>Some</u> schools have <u>bake</u> sales to raise money. <u>But</u> there are <u>other</u> ways to do that.

A. Some **B.** Bake **C.** But **D.** Other

> **Directions:** *Read the passage and answer the questions below.*

COUNTRIES OF THE WORLD: INDIA

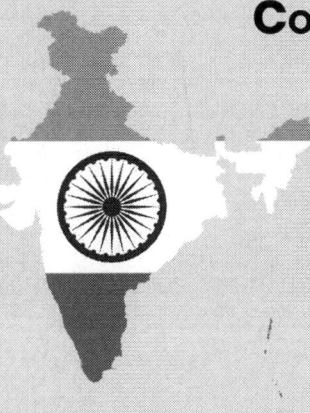

India is in South Asia. Most of the country forms a peninsula. That means it has water on three sides. In north India are the Himalayas. This is a mountain range. It is the tallest in the world. Southeast India borders the Bay of Bengal. Southwest India borders the Arabian Sea.

India is made up of different kinds of lands. Some are deserts and others are jungles. The Ganges Plain covers much of northern India. It is made up of rich soil. This soil is good for growing things.

India is home to many different animals. Elephants and rhinos live here. So do lions and tigers. It is the only country with both lions and tigers!

=== MULTIPLE CHOICE ===

7. Which sentence best introduces the topic of this text? (W.2.2)
  A. Southwest India borders the Arabian Sea.
  B. India is made up of different kinds of lands.
  C. North India contains the Himalayas.
  D. India is in South Asia.

8. Which statement is a fact? (W.2.2)
  A. India is the most exciting country in the world.
  B. India is home to many different animals.
  C. People should visit India quite often.
  D. There are too many animals in India.

4. WRITING

9. **Which sentence is a definition?** (W.2.2)

    A. That means it has water on three sides.
    B. It is the tallest in the world.
    C. This soil is good for growing things.
    D. It is the only country with both lions and tigers!

> **Directions:** *Read the passage and answer the questions below.*

DAISY DAWSON'S ON THE WAY

"Rover?" she called, opening up her lunch box. "Rover, come and see what I've got for you!"

A large, grumpy-looking bloodhound stuck his head through a hole in the bricks, blinking and sneezing in the bright sunlight.

His fur was the color of sandstone, and his serious brown eyes stared out from folds of baggy skin that hung down around his face. As he padded toward her, his long floppy ears swung back and forth, flapping up dust from the dry ground.

When he reached the gate, he stopped and looked at her expectantly. "Good morning," he said in a deep, gravelly voice. "What's on the menu today?" Daisy was so shocked that she dropped her lunch box and put a hand up to her mouth. This cannot be happening, she thought. She shut her eyes tightly for a moment or two, then opened them again.

4.1. TEXT TYPES AND PURPOSES

═══ **TRUE OR FALSE** ═══

10. **"Daisy was so shocked that she dropped her lunch box and put a hand up to her mouth."**

    This sentence gives details about the character's actions and feelings. (W.2.3)

    A. True   B. False

11. **This text narrates a long sequence of events.** (W.2.3)

    A. True   B. False

4. WRITING

12. "She shut her eyes tightly for a moment or two, then opened them again."

This sentence uses a temporal word to show event order. (W.2.3)

A. True   **B.** False

> **Directions:** *Read the passage and answer the questions below.*

Daisy Dawson's on the Way

The day was warm, and the sky was china blue. Bees buzzed among the foxgloves, and Daisy wandered down the lane, humming a little tune to herself.

Suddenly, from the corner of her eye, she caught sight of a beautiful yellow butterfly stuck in a spider's web. As she crouched down to take a closer look, a black spider emerged from beneath a leaf and began crawling across the web toward it.

"Oh, no, you don't!" said Daisy, cupping her hand protectively around the struggling insect. As the spider scuttled back to its hiding place, Daisy scooped the butterfly out of the web and carefully pulled some sticky strands from its wings.

=== MULTIPLE CHOICE ===

13. Which underlined word is a temporal word in this sentence? (W.2.3)

<u>Suddenly</u>, from the corner of <u>her</u> eye, she caught sight of a <u>beautiful</u> yellow butterfly stuck in a <u>spider's</u> web.

A. Suddenly   **B.** Her   **C.** Beautiful   **D.** Spider's

14. Which sentence does not describe the character's actions? (W.2.3)

A. Bees buzzed among the foxgloves, and Daisy wandered down the lane, humming a little tune to herself.

B. The day was warm, and the sky was china blue.

C. She crouched down to take a closer look, a black spider emerged from beneath a leaf and began crawling across the web toward it.

D. "Oh, no, you don't!" said Daisy, cupping her hand protectively around the struggling insect.

4.1. TEXT TYPES AND PURPOSES

4. WRITING

15. Which answer best describes the sequence of events in this text? (W.2.3)

   A. First Daisy scooped up the butterfly, then she wandered down the lane.
   B. First Daisy caught sight of the butterfly, then she pulled sticky strands from its wings.
   C. First Daisy crouched down to take a closer look, then she caught sight of the butterfly.
   D. First Daisy caught sight of the butterfly, she crouched down to take a closer look.

> **Directions:** *Read the passage and answer the questions below.*

Hannah looked all over for her dog, Freddy. First, she checked the backyard. Then, she checked the park. She even checked Freddy's favorite tree by the lake. But she could not find Freddy. Hannah became very sad and worried. She sat by the lake and wondered. What if Freddy was lost forever? All of a sudden, she heard something moving in the bushes. "What was that?" she said. Next, she slowly walked over to the bushes.

=== MULTIPLE CHOICE ===

16. Which sentence does not use temporal words to show event order? (W.2.3)

   A. First, she checked the backyard.
   B. Then, she checked the park.
   C. She sat by the lake and wondered.
   D. Next, she slowly walked over to the bushes.

4.1. TEXT TYPES AND PURPOSES

4. WRITING

WRITING PROMPT

17. Write an ending for this story. (W.2.3)

4. WRITING

> **Directions:** Read the passage and answer the questions below.

Spring is the best season. Some people say that it rains too much during springtime. But I disagree with them. Rain is important because it is good for plants and flowers. This is what makes spring so special. Gardens grow in the spring. Trees are beautiful and green. Animals come out from winter hibernation.

FILL IN THE BLANK

18. **Rain is important <u>because</u> it is good for plants and flowers.**

    The underlined word is an example of a _____ word in the text. (W.2.1)

19. **Spring is the best season.**

    This sentence states the author's _____ about spring. (W.2.1)

WRITING PROMPT

20. **Write a concluding statement for this text.** (W.2.1)

    _____

    _____

    _____

    _____

    _____

4.2. Chapter Review

4. WRITING

4.2. Chapter Review

Common Core State Standards: CCSS.ELA-LITERACY.W.2.1, CCSS.ELA-LITERACY.W.2.2, CCSS.ELA-LITERACY.W.2.3

Skills:
- Write opinion pieces in which they introduce the topic or book they are writing about, state an opinion, supply reasons that support the opinion, use linking words (e.g., because, and, also) to connect opinion and reason, and provide a concluding statement or section.
- Write informative/explanatory texts in which they introduce a topic, use facts and definitions to develop points, and provide a concluding statement or section.
- Write narratives in which they recount a well-elaborated event or short sequence of events, include details to describe actions, thoughts, and feelings, use temporal words to signal event order, and provide a sense of closure.

> **Direction:** Read the passage and answer the questions below.

A parakeet is a type of bird. It has a small, slim body and a long tail. Its feathers are usually yellow and green. Male parakeets have a blue cere. A cere is the skin above a parakeet's beak. Female parakeets have a tan cere. This is one way to tell males and female parakeets apart.

Parakeets are interesting. They can be taught to speak words. This is because they mimic, or copy, the sounds they hear around them. Some parakeets can say over 1,000 words! But most parakeets just repeat what people teach them. They might only say a few words. Overall, parakeets can be chatty birds.

4. WRITING

MULTIPLE CHOICE

1. **Which sentence is a definition?** (W.2.2)
   A. Parakeets have a small, slim body and a long tail.
   B. Parakeets are interesting because they can be taught to speak words.
   C. A cere is the skin above a parakeet's beak.
   D. Some parakeets can say over 1,000 words!

2. **Which sentence best introduces the topic?** (W.2.2)
   A. This is one way to tell males and female parakeets apart.
   B. This is because they mimic, or copy, the sounds they hear around them.
   C. Male parakeets have a blue cere.
   D. A parakeet is a type of bird.

3. **Which sentence is a concluding statement?** (W.2.2)
   A. Overall, parakeets can be chatty birds.
   B. Female parakeets have a tan cere.
   C. A parakeet is a type of bird.
   D. Its feathers are usually yellow and green.

4. **Which sentence is not a fact?** (W.2.2)
   A. This is because they mimic, or copy, the sounds they hear around them.
   B. Parakeets are interesting.
   C. Its feathers are usually yellow and green.
   D. A cere is the skin above a parakeet's beak.

4. WRITING

TRUE OR FALSE

5. **The words *and, also,* and *because* are examples of linking words.** (W.2.1)

    A. True   **B.** False

6. **The words *finally, before* and *later* are examples of temporal words.** (W.2.3)

    A. True   **B.** False

7. **Opinion writing is based on facts about a topic.** (W.2.1)

    A. True   **B.** False

8. **Informative texts should tell a story.** (W.2.3)

    A. True   **B.** False

> **Directions:** *Read the passage and answer the questions below.*

SLOW LORISES ARE BEING STOLEN FROM THE RAINFOREST

Slow lorises are cute animals. They have big eyes. They live in Southeast Asia. Videos of lorises are popular on the Internet. They show people tickling the animals. They also show people feeding them rice balls.

These videos are adorable. They also show a serious problem. Many people want to keep lorises as pets. But lorises are wild animals. Slow lorises live in the rainforest.

In Southeast Asia, they are supposed to be protected. Laws were set to protect wild animals. It is against the law to sell them. However, some people break these laws. Many lorises are still stolen each year. They are taken from their homes. Some are sold online. Others are sold in other countries.

4. WRITING

MULTIPLE CHOICE

9. **Which statement is not an opinion?** (W.2.2)
   - **A.** Slow lorises are cute animals.
   - **B.** These videos are adorable.
   - **C.** Slow lorises live in the rainforest.
   - **D.** All of these statements are opinions.

10. **Which sentence does not use a linking word?** (W.2.2)
    - **A.** They also show people feeding them rice balls.
    - **B.** However, some people break these laws.
    - **C.** But lorises are wild animals.
    - **D.** They are taken from their homes.

TRUE OR FALSE

11. **The author most likely has a positive opinion about slow lorises.** (W.2.1)
    - **A.** True
    - **B.** False

12. **The author mostly likely has a negative opinion about keeping lorises as pets.** (W.2.1)
    - **A.** True
    - **B.** False

> **Directions:** Read the passage and answer the questions below.

SLOW LORISES ARE BEING STOLEN FROM THE RAINFOREST

Customers love the cute animals. But lorises are not meant to be pets. They have very sharp teeth. These are taken out before the animals are sold. It causes them a lot of pain.

Then things get even worse. In 2016, scientists studied pet lorises. They looked at 100 online videos of them. The scientists found that the animals were not doing well. Some were sick. Others were very unhappy.

...continued next page

4. WRITING

> Christine Rattel is a scientist. She works for International Animal Rescue. This is a group that helps animals in danger. Ms. Rattel said that lorises are delicate. They do not like to be touched. Ms. Rattel is worried. She thinks lorises are in danger of dying out. That could happen if the pet trade continues, she said.

MULTIPLE CHOICE

13. **Which sentence best describes the author's opinion?** (W.2.2)
    - A. In 2016, scientists studied pet lorises.
    - B. But lorises are not meant to be pets.
    - C. They do not like to be touched.
    - D. This is a group that helps animals in danger.

14. **Which sentence best supports the author's opinion?** (W.2.2)
    - A. This causes them a lot of pain.
    - B. The scientists found that the animals were not doing well.
    - C. Some were sick.
    - D. All of these sentences support the author's opinion.

15. **Which sentence expresses someone else's opinion?** (W.2.2)
    - A. Christine Rattel is a scientist.
    - B. She thinks lorises are in danger of dying out.
    - C. She works for International Animal Rescue.
    - D. Then things got even worse.

16. **Which statement would best conclude this text?** (W.2.2)
    - A. All in all, lorises are cute but can attack humans.
    - B. Lastly, people should not make videos of lorises.
    - C. In conclusion, lorises are cute but do not make good pets.
    - D. As you can see, lorises have very sharp teeth.

4. WRITING

> **Directions:** Read the passage and answer the questions below.

What is it Like to Live in the Coldest Town Known to Man?

Oymyakon is a small village. About 500 people live there. It is the coldest town in the world.

In the winter it gets very cold. The temperatures drop below zero. It can be -58 degrees in winter. That is 90 degrees colder than when water turns to ice. Eyelashes freeze. People worry about frostbite. Frostbite comes from being outside in the very cold weather. It hurts the fingers, toes, and nose.

Oymyakon sits in the far north. It is near the Arctic Circle. It is close to the North Pole. Winter days are short in Oymyakon. The town is in darkness 21 hours a day. People around the world are curious about this place. How do people live in such cold weather?

=== FILL IN THE BLANK ===

17. The _____ of this text is Oymyakon, the coldest town in the world. (W.2.2)

18. It can be -58 degrees in winter.

    This sentence is a _____ used to develop the topic of the text. (W.2.2)

19. Frostbite comes from being outside in the very cold weather.

    This sentence is a _____ used to develop the topic of the text. (W.2.2)

4. WRITING

> **Directions:** *Read the passage and answer the questions below.*

Don't Look Directly At It

Looking at the sun on a normal day might make you squint, but looking at the sun during a solar eclipse will cause a lot of damage to your eyes. Have you ever heard of a solar eclipse? You might not have heard about it because they do not come around very often. The last time the United States was able to experience a solar eclipse was in August 2017. Did you see it then? It was so cool to see! If you didn't, that is okay. But, you will have to wait for the next one. The next solar eclipse will happen in the year 2042. Yes, that is a long time away!

What actually happens during a solar eclipse? The sky will get very dark. Then, the Earth will be in the direct path of the sun. This causes the sun to be very bright. The sun, Earth, and moon will all be aligned. This is just for a short period of time though. It usually takes a little over an hour. The reason that the solar eclipse does not happen all of the time is because the Earth is tilted and only aligns with the sun every twenty-five years.

If viewing a solar eclipse hurts our eyes, then how do we see it? You will need to wear special glasses in order to see a solar eclipse.When the sun is in the direct path of Earth, it will be too bright for human eyes. Scientists make special glasses you can wear to view it. Many people think that they can wear their regular sunglasses to look at a solar eclipse, but that will not work. Regular sunglasses will not protect your eyes. You can get these special glasses on the Internet. Also, during the time of a solar eclipse, many stores will sell them as well.

=== **MULTIPLE CHOICE** ===

20. Which sentence best introduces the topic in paragraph 1? (W.2.2)
   - **A.** Solar eclipses happen every twenty five years.
   - **B.** Solar eclipses happen every twenty five years.
   - **C.** You need special glasses to look at a solar eclipse.
   - **D.** The solar eclipse happens when the sun, moon, and Earth align.

4. WRITING

21. Which sentence best introduces the topic in paragraph 2? (W.2.2)
   A. You will need special glasses to look at a solar eclipse.
   B. The solar eclipse happens when the sun, moon, and Earth align.
   C. The last solar eclipse happened in 2017.
   D. The next solar eclipse will happen in 2042.

22. Which sentence(s) is not a fact? (W.2.2)
   A. The last solar eclipse happened in 2017.
   B. Solar eclipses hurt people's eyes.
   C. Did you see it then? It was so cool to see!
   D. Solar eclipses happen when the sun, Earth, and moon align.

23. Which sentence is a concluding statement? (W.2.2)
   A. So, mark your calendars for 2042 and get your solar eclipse glasses!
   B. Solar eclipses happen when the sun, Earth, and moon align.
   C. Solar eclipses cannot be view with regular sunglasses.
   D. The last solar eclipse occured in 2017.

> **Directions:** *Read the paragraph and answer the questions below.*

THE MINIATURE WORLD OF MARVIN AND JAMES

Scot was shaking in his seat. He couldn't sit still. His mind was racing. His palms were sweating. He couldn't believe he forgot. He never forgets! But he was just so busy the previous night that it just slipped his mind. Right after school yesterday Scott had football practice, which ran late. He then had to hurry to the restaurant to celebrate his little sister's fourth birthday. Then, when he got home, it was time for cake and presents. When that was over, it was very late. It was past Scot's bedtime and he went to sleep. He completely forgot that he had math homework to do.

Scot opened his bookbag, got out his math notebook, and opened it up to homework he did last week. He didn't want his teacher to know he didn't do it. He didn't want his classmates to know either. He was hoping he wouldn't be called on to demonstrate any problems on the board. He didn't want to be embarrassed.

4. WRITING

MULTIPLE CHOICE

24. Which sentence best describes the character's feelings in the text?
(W.2.3)

    A. He didn't want to be embarrassed.

    B. Scot opened his bookbag, got out his math notebook, and opened it up to homework he did last week.

    C. He completely forgot he had math homework to do.

    D. Right after school yesterday Scott had football practice, which ran late.

25. Which sentence best describes the character's actions in the text?
(W.2.3)

    A. He didn't want to be embarrassed.

    B. Scot opened his bookbag, got out his math notebook, and opened it up to homework he did last week.

    C. He completely forgot he had math homework to do.

    D. His palms were sweating.

> **Directions:** Read the passage and answer the questions below.

Prize Winning Day

    Amanda waited all day for this moment. In fact, she waited the entire year for this moment. Actually, she waited almost her entire life for this moment. Amanda had been riding horses ever since she was old enough to sit up. She spent countless hours in the barn bonding with her horse, running her horse, and practicing the course. This was the day she could let the world know how much she wants to win and the talent she has.

    Amanda brushed Lucky till she shined. She also put her little pink bow in her mane. Lucky likes her bow. When Amanda puts it on her, Lucky knows that it is competition time. Amanda waited till the last minute before getting into her uniform. She bought a new one, and she didn't want to get it dirty. She really wanted to look nice and impress the judges because one portion of the score is rider and horse presentation.

4. WRITING

> When it was time, Amanda's trainer told Amanda to get ready. Amanda slowly climbed on Lucky. She gave her a couple pats on the back, some pets, and then whispered into her ear. She said, "We got this."
>
> Then, the bell ran. Amanda and Lucky were off. They jumped and jumped over the miniature fences with precision and speed. At the end of the day, after everyone performed, the judges met and decided that Amanda was the winner. She had the highest score. She won a blue ribbon and a trophy that was so big she was unsure how it would fit in her dad's car. Amanda wanted to share her prizes with Lucky as she couldn't have done this without him, but Lucky did not care about her blue ribbon or her trophy. Lucky wanted a carrot!

MULTIPLE CHOICE

26. Which sentence uses a transition word to show event order? (W.2.3)

- **A.** Lucky wanted a carrot!
- **B.** Then, the bell ran.
- **C.** She really wanted to look nice and impress the judges because one portion of the score is rider and horse presentation.
- **D.** She said, "We got this."

27. Which sentence describes the character's thoughts in the text? (W.2.3)

- **A.** Amanda brushed Lucky till she shined.
- **B.** She really wanted to look nice and impress the judges because one portion of the score is rider and horse presentation.
- **C.** When it was time, Amanda's trainer told Amanda to get ready.
- **D.** Actually, she waited almost her entire life for this moment.

TRUE OR FALSE

28. This story describes a detailed sequence of events. (W.2.3)

- **A.** True
- **B.** False

29. This story does not describe the character's actions. (W.2.3)

- **A.** True
- **B.** False

4. WRITING

> **Directions:** *Read the passage and answer the questions below.*

THE STORY OF BOOKS

Long ago, people learned stories by heart. There were no books to read from. People told poems and stories to each other. There were many stories to share. It was hard to remember them all.

Writing changed this. It made it much easier to share stories with others.

The first writers used sticks. They made marks in soft clay. The clay became hard and strong when it dried.

At first, writing was just used to keep lists. Soon people recorded other information. For example, poets could now write down poems. Storytellers could write down their stories.

=== MULTIPLE CHOICE ===

30. What is the topic of this text? (W.2.2)
- **A.** Ways to record information
- **B.** The history of writing stories
- **C.** Famous storytellers
- **D.** Ancient poetry

5. LANGUAGE

5.1. CONVENTIONS OF STANDARD ENGLISH   140
- Conventions of grammar
- Conventions of punctuation
- Conventions of spelling

5.2. KNOWLEDGE OF LANGUAGE   144
- Conventions of speaking and writing

5.3. VOCABULARY ACQUISITION AND USE   148
- Multiple meaning words
- Word relationships and nuances

5.4. CHAPTER REVIEW   152

5. LANGUAGE

5.1. Conventions of Standard English

Common Core State Standards: CCSS.ELA-LITERACY.L.2.1, CCSS.ELA-LITERACY.L.2.2

Skills:
- Demonstrate command of the conventions of standard English grammar and usage when writing or speaking
- Demonstrate command of the conventions of standard English capitalization, punctuation, and spelling when writing

=== EXAMPLE QUESTION ===

> **Directions:** *Complete the sentence below with the correct collective noun.*

E1 I saw a _____ of fish swimming in the same direction. (L.2.1)

    A. Group   **B.** School   **C.** Pack   **D.** Flock

Answer: **B.** The word school is the correct collective noun to describe a collection of fish.

=== EXAMPLE QUESTION ===

> **Directions:** *Circle the words that should be capitalized in the sentences below. Then rewrite each sentence in the correct way.*

E2 This (thursday) is (thanksgiving), so we don't have to go to class. (L.2.2)

Correct Answer: **This Thursday is Thanksgiving, so we don't have to go to class.** Thursday is a day of the week and Thanksgiving is a holiday so both need to be capitalized.

5. LANGUAGE

MULTIPLE CHOICE

> **Directions:** Complete the sentences below with the correct collective noun.

1. The _____ of elephants were marching. (L.2.1)
   A. Group **B.** Herd **C.** Pack **D.** Flock

2. We should go on vacation as a _____. (L.2.1)
   A. Herd **B.** School **C.** Group **D.** Pack

3. Pick the sentence with the apostrophe in the correct place. (L.2.2)
   A. I dont wan't to go to the mall tomorrow.
   B. I don't want to go to the mall tomorrow.
   C. I do'nt want to go to the mall tomorrow.
   D. I dont' want to go to the mall tomorrow.

4. Pick the sentence with the apostrophe in the correct place. (L.2.2)
   A. Shell wish she went with us.
   B. Sh'ell wish she went with us.
   C. She'll wish she went with us.
   D. Shell' wish she went with us.

5. Pick the sentence with the correct contraction for will not. (L.2.2)
   A. will'nt **B.** won't **C.** will **D.** wi'll

6. Pick the sentence with the correct contraction for cannot. (L.2.2)
   A. can'not **B.** cann'ot **C.** can't **D.** cant

7. Pick the sentence with the correct contraction for I am. (L.2.2)
   A. I'am **B.** I'a **C.** I'm **D.** I am'

5.1. CONVENTIONS OF STANDARD ENGLISH

5. LANGUAGE

> **Directions:** *Complete the sentences below with the correct irregular plural noun.*

8. **I forgot to wear my socks, so my _____ were cold all day.** (L.2.1)
    A. Shoes   B. Foot   C. Foots   D. Feet

9. **I bit into my ice cream, so my two front _____ hurt.** (L.2.1)
    A. Tooth   B. Tooths   C. Toothes   D. Teeth

> **Directions:** *Complete the sentences below with the correct reflexive pronoun.*

10. **I can reach the top drawer _____.** (L.2.1)
    A. Ourselves
    B. Myself
    C. Themselves
    D. Himself

11. **We decided to help _____ because nobody was home.** (L.2.1)
    A. Ourselves
    B. Myself
    C. Themselves
    D. Herself

> **Directions:** *Complete the sentence below with the correct past tense form of the irregular verb.*

12. **The chair was too small, so Jake _____ on the couch.** (L.2.1)
    A. Sit   B. Sat   C. Sits   D. Sats

> **Directions:** *Complete the sentences below with the correct adverb.*

13. **I placed the glass bowl down _____.** (L.2.1)
    A. Careful   B. Carefully   C. Care   D. Cares

5.1. CONVENTIONS OF STANDARD ENGLISH

NAME: _____ DATE: _____ 143

5. LANGUAGE

14. **Pick the word that is spelled correctly.** (L.2.2)
    A. bage **B.** bagge **C.** badeg **D.** badge

15. **Pick the word that is spelled correctly.** (L.2.2)
    A. flaor **B.** flaar **C.** flavr **D.** flavor

═══════════ **FREE RESPONSE** ═══════════

> **Directions:** *Circle all the adjectives that appear in the sentences below.*

16. **The bright, red car drove fast around the block.** (L.2.1)

17. **I climbed a rocky mountain with my brother.** (L.2.1)

> **Directions:** *Circle the words that should be capitalized in the sentences below. Then rewrite each sentence in the correct way.*

18. **My brother, timothy, wants a nike jacket for his birthday.** (L.2.2)
    _____

19. **We celebrate halloween on october 31st.** (L.2.2)
    _____

20. **Last summer I went to texas and florida with my family.** (L.2.2)
    _____

5.1. CONVENTIONS OF STANDARD ENGLISH

5.2. KNOWLEDGE OF LANGUAGE

www.prepaze.com   Copyrighted Material

5. LANGUAGE

5.2. Knowledge of Language

Common Core State Standards: CCSS.ELA-LITERACY.L.2.3

Skills:
- Use knowledge of language and its conventions when writing, speaking, reading, or listening

=== **EXAMPLE QUESTION** ===

> **Directions:** *Read the sentence below. Determine whether the sentence is written in formal or informal English.*

E1 **This sentence is written in formal English: "Thank you, sir."**

    A. True   **B.** False

Answer: **A.** The sentence is written in formal English because it uses a proper form of gratitude and a formal address by using the word "sir".

=== **TRUE OR FALSE** ===

> **Directions:** *Read the sentences below. Determine whether each sentence is written in formal or informal English.*

1. **This sentence is written in formal English: "Thanks, girl!"** (L.2.3)

    A. True   **B.** False

2. **This sentence is written in informal English: "Dude, that was some party!"** (L.2.3)

    A. True   **B.** False

5. LANGUAGE

3. **This sentence is written in informal English: "How are you?"** (L.2.3)
   - **A.** True
   - **B.** False

4. **This sentence is written in formal English: "Yo, what up?"** (L.2.3)
   - **A.** True
   - **B.** False

5. **This sentence is written in formal English: "Can you help me, please?"** (L.2.3)
   - **A.** True
   - **B.** False

6. **This sentence is written in informal English: "LOL! That was sooo cool!"** (L.2.3)
   - **A.** True
   - **B.** False

7. **This sentence is written in informal English: "What are we having for dinner tonight?"** (L.2.3)
   - **A.** True
   - **B.** False

8. **Formal English should be used when we write papers in school.** (L.2.3)
   - **A.** True
   - **B.** False

9. **Formal English should be used when we are talking to a teacher, police officer, or librarian.** (L.2.3)
   - **A.** True
   - **B.** False

10. **Informal English should only be spoken.** (L.2.3)
    - **A.** True
    - **B.** False

5. LANGUAGE

MULTIPLE CHOICE

> **Directions:** *Answer the questions below with the best possible choice.*

11. Pick the sentence that uses formal English. (L.2.3)
   A. I like to go to the beach with my friends.
   B. I kinda like to go to the beach with my friends.
   C. Man, I really like to go to the beach with my friends.
   D. I like to go to the beach with my peeps.

12. Pick the sentence that uses informal English. (L.2.3)
   A. He had to stay up all night to study.
   B. She had to stay up all night to study.
   C. We had to stay up all night to study.
   D. Dude, I had to stay up all night to study.

13. Pick the sentence that uses informal English. (L.2.3)
   A. That place was totally cool.
   B. That place was really neat.
   C. That place was really nice.
   D. That place was really fun.

14. Pick the sentence that uses formal English. (L.2.3)
   A. Haha!
   B. Oh man!
   C. That was so funny!
   D. LOL!

15. What are some similarities between formal and informal English? (L.2.3)
   A. We use both formal and informal English when we speak on the phone.
   B. Formal and informal English can be used at any time.
   C. Formal and informal English are the same thing.
   D. We use both formal and informal English when we give a speech.

5. LANGUAGE

16. **What are some differences between formal and informal English?** (L.2.3)
    - **A.** Formal English is only used when we speak in public.
    - **B.** Informal English is only used when we speak in public.
    - **C.** We use formal English to write and speak properly and informal English when we talk to people we feel comfortable with like our friends.
    - **D.** Informal English should never be used.

=== FREE RESPONSE ===

> **Directions:** *Read the sentences below. Rewrite each sentence to either formal or informal English.*

17. **Rewrite the sentence to formal English: "Yo, let's go before we're late!"** (L.2.3)
    _____

18. **Rewrite the sentence to formal English: "Man, what's going on?"** (L.2.3)
    _____

19. **Rewrite the sentence to informal English: "Can you hear me?"** (L.2.3)
    _____

20. **Rewrite the sentence to informal English: "Where are we going?"** (L.2.3)
    _____

5.3. Vocabulary Acquisition and Use

5. LANGUAGE

5.3. Vocabulary Acquisition and Use

Common Core State Standards: CCSS.ELA-LITERACY.L.2.4, CCSS.ELA-LITERACY.L.2.5

Skills:
- Determine or clarify the meaning of unknown and multiple-meaning words and phrases based on grade 2 reading and content, choosing flexibly from an array of strategies
- Demonstrate an understanding of word relationships and nuances in word meanings

=== EXAMPLE QUESTION ===

➤ **Directions:** Read the sentence below. Determine the meaning of the underlined word.

E1 I had to <u>retell</u> the story because she didn't hear it the first time. (L.2.4)

    A. Say aloud   **B.** Read   **C.** Tell again   **D.** Speak softly

Answer: **C.** The meaning of the word <u>retell</u> is to tell again.

=== EXAMPLE QUESTION ===

➤ **Directions:** Read the word below. Choose the real-life connection that best matches the word to its use.

E2 **Ruler** (L.2.5)

    A. eat   **B.** think   **C.** comb   **D.** measure with

Answer: **D.** The meaning of the word <u>ruler</u> is to measure with.

5. LANGUAGE

MULTIPLE CHOICE

> **Directions:** Read the sentences below. Determine the meaning of the underlined word.

1. Whenever I am on the basketball court, I close my eyes and <u>imagine</u> there is a big crowd cheering for me! (L.2.4)
   - **A.** Guess
   - **B.** Dream
   - **C.** Know
   - **D.** Think

2. The <u>appearance</u> of the dusty, scratched book made it seem very old. (L.2.4)
   - **A.** Smell
   - **B.** Color
   - **C.** Look
   - **D.** Size

3. I was <u>incorrect</u> when I thought the party was yesterday. It's today. (L.2.4)
   - **A.** Right
   - **B.** Wrong
   - **C.** Fast
   - **D.** Smart

4. I <u>misspoke</u> yesterday. I didn't mean what I said. (L.2.4)
   - **A.** Spoke fast
   - **B.** Spoke slow
   - **C.** Spoke wrong or incorrectly
   - **D.** Spoke softly

> **Directions:** Read the words below. Choose the real-life connection that best matches the word to its use.

5. **Umbrella** (L.2.5)
   - **A.** carry
   - **B.** keep dry from the rain
   - **C.** swing
   - **D.** hold

6. **Orange** (L.2.5)
   - **A.** smell
   - **B.** draw with
   - **C.** look at
   - **D.** eat

7. **Shoes** (L.2.5)
   - **A.** sleep with
   - **B.** walk in
   - **C.** hold
   - **D.** make

5.3. VOCABULARY ACQUISITION AND USE

5. LANGUAGE

> **Directions:** Read the definitions below. Determine the meaning of the underlined word.

8. *Addition* is a word used when two or more things are put together to increase or have more of something. What does the word <u>additional</u> mean? (L.2.4)

    A. Add on, extra
    B. Too much
    C. More
    D. Many things

9. *Careful* is a word used when someone tries to avoid harm by paying attention. What does the word <u>careless</u> mean? (L.2.4)

    A. Carefully
    B. Slowly
    C. Caring
    D. Thoughtless

> **Directions:** Read the following sentences and circle the best answer choice.

10. **Circle the word that is not a *spicy* food.** (L.2.5)

    A. Pepper
    B. Jalapeno
    C. Chili
    D. Apple

11. **Circle the word that is not a *juicy* food.** (L.2.5)

    A. Watermelon
    B. Strawberry
    C. Corn
    D. Apple

=== TRUE OR FALSE ===

> **Directions:** Read the definitions below for each of the compound words. Determine if the given meaning of the underlined word is true or false.

12. The definition of the word <u>birdhouse</u> is: A shelter for birds that contains bird seed. (L.2.4)

    A. True
    B. False

13. The definition of the word <u>lighthouse</u> is: A house that is painted white. (L.2.4)

    A. True
    B. False

5. LANGUAGE

> **Directions:** Read the definitions below for each of the vocabulary words. Determine if the given meaning of the underlined word is true or false.

14. The definition of the word <u>ridiculous</u> is: Something that is silly. (L.2.4)

  A. True **B.** False

15. The definition of the word <u>diagram</u> is: A tall building. (L.2.4)

  A. True **B.** False

> **Directions:** Read the underlined verbs below. Determine if the verb best describes the category listed by marking true or false.

16. The verb <u>toss</u> describes the category *to throw*. (L.2.5)

  A. True **B.** False

17. The verb <u>pitch</u> describes the category *to throw*. (L.2.5)

  A. True **B.** False

18. The verb <u>capture</u> describes the category *to catch*. (L.2.5)

  A. True **B.** False

> **Directions:** Read the underlined adjectives below. Determine if the adjective best describes the category listed by marking true or false.

19. The adjective <u>slim</u> describes the category *thick*. (L.2.5)

  A. True **B.** False

20. The adjective <u>scrawny</u> describes the category *thin*. (L.2.5)

  A. True **B.** False

5.4. CHAPTER REVIEW

5. LANGUAGE

5.4. Chapter Review

=== MULTIPLE CHOICE ===

> **Directions:** *Complete the sentence below with the correct collective noun.*

1. We heard a _____ of wolves howling. (L.2.1)
   - **A.** Group
   - **B.** Herd
   - **C.** Flock
   - **D.** Pack

> **Directions:** *Read the words below. Choose the real-life connection that best matches the word to its use.*

2. **Pencil** (L.2.5)
   - **A.** buy
   - **B.** paint with
   - **C.** draw with
   - **D.** color

3. **Desk** (L.2.5)
   - **A.** read
   - **B.** write on
   - **C.** measure with
   - **D.** carry

4. **Song** (L.2.5)
   - **A.** sing
   - **B.** make
   - **C.** learn
   - **D.** read

> **Directions:** *Read the sentences below. Determine the meaning of the underlined word.*

5. She <u>cautiously</u> helped her mom crack the eggs because she didn't want to drop any on the floor. (L.2.4)
   - **A.** Carefully
   - **B.** Quickly
   - **C.** Easily
   - **D.** Thoughtlessly

NAME: _____ DATE: _____

5. LANGUAGE

6. **When our house burned down, a fireman was able to <u>rescue</u> our dog, Max.** (L2.4)
   - **A.** See
   - **B.** Save
   - **C.** Catch
   - **D.** Pet

7. **I <u>dislike</u> tomatoes. I won't eat them if they are on my pizza.** (L2.4)
   - **A.** Don't like
   - **B.** Like very much
   - **C.** Love
   - **D.** Confused

> **Directions:** Complete the sentence below with the correct irregular plural noun.

8. **The playground was loud with all the _____ yelling outside.** (L2.1)
   - **A.** Child
   - **B.** Childs
   - **C.** Children
   - **D.** Childes

> **Directions:** Complete the sentence below with the correct reflexive pronoun.

9. **They ate all the food _____.** (L2.1)
   - **A.** Ourselves
   - **B.** Myself
   - **C.** Themselves
   - **D.** Herself

10. **Pick the sentence with the apostrophe in the correct place.** (L2.2)
    - **A.** Ms. Smiths textbook is heavy.
    - **B.** Ms. Smiths' textbook is heavy.
    - **C.** Ms. Smith's textbook is heavy.
    - **D.** Ms. Smiths" textbook is heavy.

11. **Pick the sentence with the apostrophe in the correct place.** (L2.2)
    - **A.** They couldn't make the game tonight.
    - **B.** They couldnt' make the game tonight.
    - **C.** They could'nt make the game tonight.
    - **D.** They coul'dnt make the game tonight.

12. **Pick the sentence with the correct contraction for we will.** (L2.2)
    - **A.** we won't
    - **B.** well'
    - **C.** wel'l
    - **D.** we'll

5. LANGUAGE

> **Directions:** Read the definitions below. Determine the meaning of the underlined word.

13. *Pretest* is a word used when a test is taken for practice before a lesson is given. What does the word underlined posttest mean? (L.2.4)

    A. First test
    B. Second test
    C. Test taken after a lesson
    D. New test

14. *Agree* is a word used when a person likes or accepts something. What does the word underlined disagree mean? (L.2.4)

    A. Don't agree or approve
    B. Agree
    C. Work together
    D. Vote

> **Directions:** Complete the sentences below with the correct past tense form of the irregular verb.

15. Jerry was chasing his sister because she had _____ his baseball glove. (L.2.1)

    A. Hid B. Hide C. Hidden D. Hides

16. The teacher _____ them to slow down. (L.2.1)

    A. Tell B. Told C. Tells D. Talk

> **Directions:** Complete the sentences below with the correct adverb.

17. The frosting was _____ spread on the cake. (L.2.1)

    A. Even B. Evens C. Evenly D. Ever

18. We _____ ran home after school. (L.2.1)

    A. Quickly B. Quick C. Quicks D. Quicker

19. Pick the word that is spelled correctly. (L.2.2)

    A. craft B. crat C. craf D. craff

5. LANGUAGE

20. Pick the word that is spelled correctly. (L.2.2)

    A. swep   **B.** swepp   **C.** sweep   **D.** sweepp

TRUE OR FALSE

> **Directions:** Read the underlined adjectives below. Determine if the adjective best describes the category listed by marking true or false.

21. The adjective <u>chunky</u> describes the category *thick*. (L.2.5)

    A. True   **B.** False

22. The adjective <u>bulky</u> describes the category *thin*. (L.2.5)

    A. True   **B.** False

> **Directions:** Read the definitions below for each of the vocabulary words. Determine if the given meaning of the underlined word is true or false.

23. The definition of the word <u>triumph</u> is "a victory or win." (L.2.4)

    A. True   **B.** False

24. The definition of the word <u>origin</u> is "the ending of something." (L.2.4)

    A. True   **B.** False

> **Directions:** Read the underlined verbs below. Determine if the verb best describes the category listed by marking true or false.

25. The verb <u>drop</u> describes the category *to throw*. (L.2.5)

    A. True   **B.** False

5. LANGUAGE

26. The verb <u>grab</u> describes the category *to catch*. (L.2.5)

   A. True   B. False

27. The verb <u>fling</u> describes the category *to catch*. (L.2.5)

   A. True   B. False

FREE RESPONSE

> **Directions:** *Circle all the adjectives that appear in the sentence below.*

28. The caramel ice cream was sweet and creamy. (L.2.1)

> **Directions:** *Circle the words that should be capitalized in the sentences below. Then rewrite each sentence in the correct way.*

29. I was so hungry I asked my mom for mcdonalds for dinner. (L.2.2)

   _____

   _____

30. Someday I hope to travel to california to see disneyland. (L.2.2)

   _____

   _____

END OF YEAR ASSESSMENT

END OF YEAR ASSESSMENT

> **Directions:** *Read the passage and answer the questions below.*

THE STORY OF BOOKS

Early books had a big problem. Each one had to be copied by hand. This made books very beautiful. However, it also made them rare. They were expensive, too. Making a book took a long time. It was a lot of work.

The Chinese found a way to speed things up. They took a block of wood. They carved words and pictures into the block. Then they spread ink on it. They pressed the block onto paper. In this way, a whole page could be printed easily. It did not have to be copied word by word.

=== **MULTIPLE CHOICE** ===

1. **Which sentence is not a fact?** (W.2.2)
    A. They carved words and pictures into the block.
    B. Each one had to be copied by hand.
    C. This made books very beautiful.
    D. They did not have to be copied word by word.

2. **Which sentence is explanatory, or explains how to do something?** (W.2.2)
    A. They took a block of wood.
    B. Then they spread ink on it.
    C. They pressed the block onto paper.
    D. All of the above.

> **Directions:** *Read the passage and answer the questions below.*

THE TIME MACHINE

"So you're telling me this is a time machine?" Eric asked.

"Yes," his Uncle Joseph replied. "I've been working on it for years here in my lab."

...continued next page

END OF YEAR ASSESSMENT

Eric looked around the lab. A bank of computers lined one of the walls. Metal shelves held bottles and jars filled with strange liquids. There was a big metal table in the middle of the room. There were wires and tiny machine parts scattered all over it. In the middle of the bale was a silver box. The box had a small computer screen and keyboard on its face.

"All you do is type in the time you want to go to," Uncle Joseph said. "The box will transport anyone within ten feet to that location."

"So you mean if you typed in yesterday's date, it would send us back to yesterday?" Eric asked.

Uncle Joseph nodded. "Yes. But it can do better than that. I could type in 150 million years BC, for example." He typed in the date on the keyboard.

"Cool," Eric said. "And then you just press this button?" Eric put his finger on the button.

"Eric, no!" Uncle Joseph cried. But he was too late. Eric pressed the button.

The room began to spin. When everything settled, they were no longer in the lab. Tall, green plants grew all around them. A volcano rose up in the distance. Then the ground began to rumble. A huge dinosaur stomped toward them!

"Hey, a Brontosaurus!" Eric said. "Your time machine really works!"

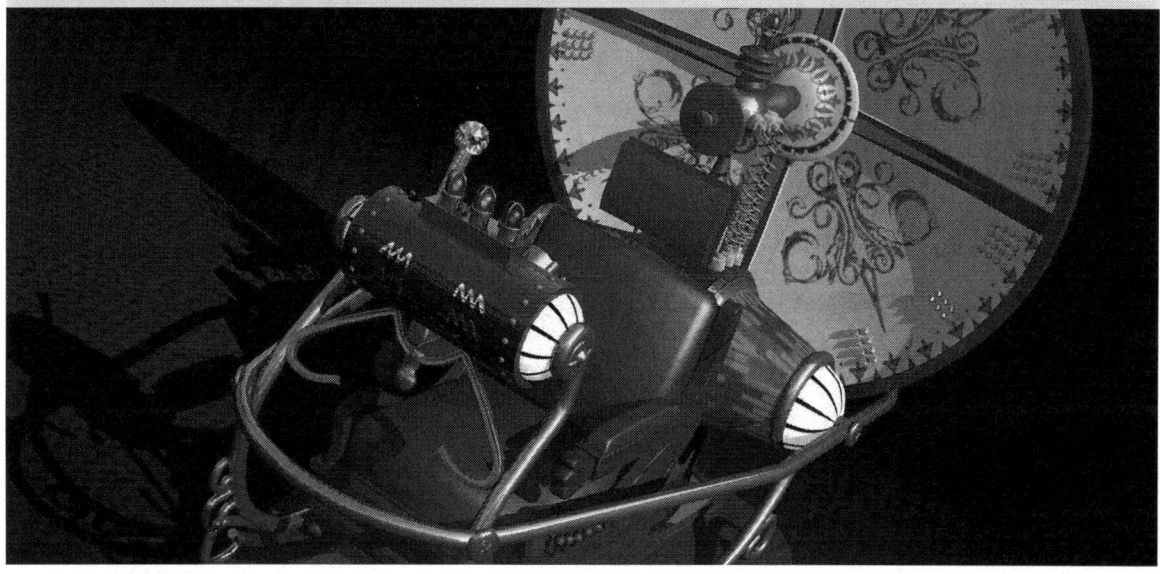

160 NAME: _____ DATE: _____

END OF YEAR ASSESSMENT

FREE RESPONSE

3. **Why does Uncle Joseph tell Eric, "it can do better than that"?** (RL.2.1)

   _____

   _____

   _____

   _____

FILL IN THE BLANK

4. **What does Eric see in 150 million BC? Eric sees** _____. (RL.2.1)

> **Directions:** *Read the articles and answer the questions below.*

KEEPING TRADITIONS ALIVE
WEEKLY READER INTERVIEWS A NATIVE AMERICAN ARTIST.

Jody Naranjo (nah-RON-hoh) is a potter. She makes pots out of clay. Her mother, grandmother, and aunts make pottery too. Naranjo is a Native American from the Santa Clara Pueblo group. She lives in New Mexico. Her work can be seen in museums across the country. Naranjo enjoys being a potter. "It's a fun job," she says. She plans to teach pottery to her daughters, ages 4, 11, and 17. "I want to keep the tradition going," she adds. A **tradition** is an idea or a way of life handed down from the past.

MANY GROUPS, MANY TRADITIONS

About 4½ million people in the United States are Native American. They live in cities and towns across the country. Some Native Americans live on **reservations**. A reservation is a land set aside for Native Americans by the U.S. government. Native Americans belong to more than 500 different groups. Each group has its own traditions.

...continued next page

NAME: .... DATE: ....

END OF YEAR ASSESSMENT

MAKING POTTERY

What is the job of a potter? Many Native American potters like Jody Narango do not purchase their material from a store. They do not order clay at a store or off of the Internet. They find their clay in the ground. This can be very difficult, but you have to know exactly what you are looking for. Native American potters dig in the ground and find the certain type of clay they are looking for. They mix different kinds of clay together to get the prefix mixture that will work best for them and for their particular project. The potters are looking for a type of clay that is strong and something that molds well.

When the potters find the clay they are looking for they use their special machines to roll out the clay in a circular fashion to make vases, bowls, pots, and cups. When the potters are finished molding their clay to their desired shape, they put their creations in the oven. This makes the clay get hard. Then, the potters decorate and paint their art.

=== FREE RESPONSE ===

5. What is the main purpose of this text? (RI.2.6)

_____

_____

_____

_____

=== MULTIPLE CHOICE ===

6. Which statement best supports the author's claim that Jody Naranjo wants "to keep the tradition going"? (RI.2.8)

  A. "She plans to teach pottery to her daughters."
  B. "She digs three different clays out of the ground and mixes them together."
  C. "Naranjo enjoys being a potter."
  D. "She finds her clay in the ground."

END OF YEAR ASSESSMENT

> **Directions:** Read the passage and answer the questions below.

THE STORY OF BOOKS

Another invention changed bookmaking about 550 years ago. It was a new kind of printing press. A man named Johannes Gutenberg invented it. His printing press used moveable letters. Printers could arrange them any way they wanted. They could be used to print copy after copy. Afterward, the same letters could be used again. They would be rearranged to make a new page. What a time saver!

The printing press made books cheaper. It also made them faster to produce. More people learned to read. Printed pictures helped them follow a story. They could tell what was happening even if they didn't know all the words.

In the past, books were only for rich people. The printing press changed that. It made books a treasure everyone could enjoy.

MULTIPLE CHOICE

7. **Which sentence best introduces the topic of this text?** (W.2.2)
   A. Printed pictures helped them follow a story.
   B. In the past, books were only for rich people.
   C. Another invention changed bookmaking about 550 years ago.
   D. More people learned to read.

8. **Which sentence is a concluding statement?** (W.2.2)
   A. The printing press made books a treasure everyone could enjoy.
   B. This was a new kind of printing press.
   C. They could be used to print copy after copy.
   D. They would be rearranged to make a new page.

END OF YEAR ASSESSMENT

TRUE OR FALSE

9. **A good opinion piece does not include supporting reasons.** (W.2.1)
   - **A.** True
   - **B.** False

10. **Linking words can be used to connect opinions and reasons.** (W.2.1)
    - **A.** True
    - **B.** False

> **Directions:** Complete the sentence below with the correct collective noun.

11. **There was a _____ of seagulls at the beach.** (L.2.1)
    - **A.** School
    - **B.** Flock
    - **C.** Group
    - **D.** Pack

> **Directions:** Complete the sentence below with the correct irregular plural noun.

12. **We found our cat chasing a pair of _____.** (L.2.1)
    - **A.** Mice
    - **B.** Mouse
    - **C.** Mices
    - **D.** Mouses

> **Directions:** Read the poem and answer the questions below.

LUNCHTIME

I love when it is lunchtime.
I get to open my lunch bag
And see all the food that's mine.
My favorite food to eat is pizza

With lots of melted cheese.
The food I hate the most
Would have to be green peas!
I always drink ice-cold milk

...continued next page

END OF YEAR ASSESSMENT

To wash my food down.
I like to add chocolate sauce,
Which makes the milk turn brown.
Sitting at the lunch table is fun,

My friends are all so silly.
We all eat together,
Sandy, Ashley, me, and Billy.
Every day at noon,

We gather in the cafeteria.
All in all, I have to say,
Lunchtime
Is my favorite time of day!

=== MULTIPLE CHOICE ===

13. Which of the words or phrases below does not describe the milk in the poem? (RL.2.4)

    A. ice-cold   **B.** chocolate sauce
    C. milk turn brown   **D.** favorite food

14. Which of these words in the poem rhymes with *silly*? (RL.2.4)

    A. fun   **B.** Billy   **C.** together   **D.** pizza

Copyrighted Material   www.prepaze.com

END OF YEAR ASSESSMENT

FREE RESPONSE

> **Directions:** Circle the words that should be capitalized in the sentences below. Then rewrite each sentence in the correct way.

15. My grandparents live in st. louis, Missouri. (L.2.2)

_____

_____

16. We celebrate easter in either the month of march or april. (L.2.2)

_____

_____

> **Directions:** Read the article and answer the question below.

Canaima National Park

Have you ever heard of a dodo bird? Some people may have never heard of this animal, and that is because this animal no longer exists. The reason why you do not see this type of bird out in the wild or even in zoos is because the dodo bird is extinct. The word extinct means that the species no longer exists or is alive. Even scientists do not know much information about this type of bird because it went into extinction many years ago. The dodo species was thought to be extinct in the year 1680.

Scientists do not know much about this type of bird, but they do know that the dodo bird lived on and near Mauritius Island. Scientists say that there are two main reasons why the dodo bird became extinct. The first reason they think the dodo bird became extinct was due to predators killing the dodo bird. The second reason why scientists think that the dodo bird went extinct is because many people on the island ate dodo birds. The dodo bird was similar to chicken. Everyone ate them. Families would go out and hunt a dodo bird, and then eat it that night for supper.

END OF YEAR ASSESSMENT

FREE RESPONSE

17. How does the author support the claim that the dodo bird became extinct? (RI.2.8)

_____
_____
_____
_____
_____

> **Directions:** Read the passage and answer the questions below.

THE ANTS AND THE GRASSHOPPER

One bright day in late autumn a family of Ants were bustling about in the warm sunshine, drying out the grain they had stored up during the summer, when a starving Grasshopper, his fiddle under his arm, came up and humbly begged for a bite to eat.

"What!" cried the Ants in surprise. "Haven't you stored anything away for the winter? What in the world were you doing all last summer?"

"I didn't have time to store up any food," whined the Grasshopper. "I was so busy making music that before I knew it the summer was gone."

The Ants shrugged their shoulders in disgust.

"Making music, were you?" they cried. "Very well; now dance!" And they turned their backs on the Grasshopper and went on with their work.

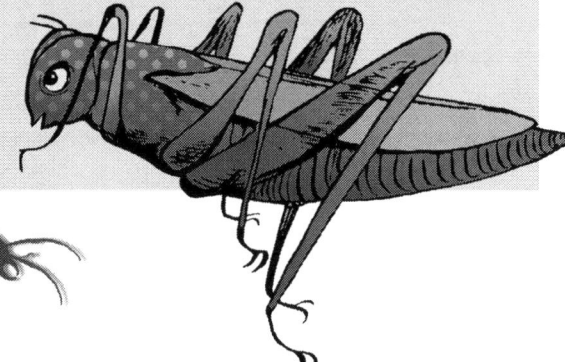

NAME: _____ DATE: _____

END OF YEAR ASSESSMENT

FREE RESPONSE

18. What is the lesson of the story? (RL.2.2)

_____

_____

_____

_____

_____

FILL IN THE BLANK

19. The Ants spent the summer getting ready for _____. (RL.2.2)

> **Directions:** Read the articles and answer the questions below.

ARTICLE 1 IN MEMORY OF DR. KING

A piece of the nation's capital will honor an important leader—Dr. Martin Luther King Jr. A memorial for King is being built on the National Mall in Washington, D.C. It will be the first memorial on the Mall to honor an African American.

A ceremony was held on November 13, [2006] to mark the start of construction. President George W. Bush and other leaders were among the thousands of people who gathered for the event.

"When the work is done, the King memorial will be a fitting tribute—powerful and hopeful and poetic—like the man it honors," Bush said at the ceremony.

...continued next page

END OF YEAR ASSESSMENT

> ### ARTICLE 2 HONORING A GREAT AMERICAN
>
> Dr. King is honored with a **memorial**. A memorial is a statue or a place that honors a person or an event. The King Memorial is built on the National Mall. That is a park in Washington, D.C., our nation's capital. Memorials for some U.S. presidents are also on the Mall.
>
> The King Memorial opened in August of 2011. It has a 30-foot statue of King. Sentences from some of his speeches are carved into a stone wall.
>
> The cost of the memorial was $100 million. A concert was held in September 2010 in New York City to raise some of the money. Many famous singers performed. The singers included Aretha Franklin, Stevie Wonder, and Garth Brooks.

TRUE OR FALSE

20. **If a reader wants to learn about when construction on the King Memorial started they should read Article 1.** (RI.2.9)

    A. True   **B.** False

FILL IN THE BLANK

21. **If a reader wants to learn about how the King Memorial was paid for they should read Article** __2__ . (RI.2.9)

MULTIPLE CHOICE

> **Directions:** *Read the sentence below. Determine the meaning of the underlined word.*

22. **David was <u>unhappy</u> because his video game broke.** (L.2.4)

    A. Happy   **B.** Scared   **C.** Sad   **D.** Hurt

END OF YEAR ASSESSMENT

TRUE OR FALSE

> **Directions:** *Read the definition below for the compound words. Determine if the given meaning of the underlined word is true or false.*

23. The definition of the word <u>bookshelf</u> is: Office furniture for holding books. (L.2.4)

    A. True   **B.** False

> **Directions:** *Read the passage and answer the questions below.*

MOVING DAY

On Saturday afternoon, Julia spotted the moving truck outside of her bedroom window. It was finally moving day.

Julia let out a sigh. She looked around her room at her toys spread out on the floor. Julia grabbed an empty box and began packing up her toys.

"Are you almost ready to go?" called her mom.

Julia moved quickly to grab the rest of her toys. "Yes!" she said.

When everything in her room was gone, Julia stood in the middle of the floor. She looked around at the walls and windows. She just stood there quietly remembering all the fun times she had in her room. She felt a tear on her cheek.

Julia walked over to the light switch and turned off the lights for the last time. She closed the door and headed out of her old house. Her mom was outside with the moving truck.

"Let's hurry and get to the new house before it gets too dark," said her mom.

Julia got in the car and drove with her mom over to their new house.

"Here it is!" said her mom. "Julia, you are going to love it here. I know you loved your old room, but your new room is much bigger."

...continued next page

Julia slowly walked into the new house. Her mom pointed to the door of her new room. As Julia opened the door, a big smile came across her face. Her mom was right. This room was much bigger than her old one. It had more windows, too. The walls were painted bright pink. This was her favorite color. Julia would feel right at home here.

MULTIPLE CHOICE

24. What happens in the middle of the story? (RL.2.5)
   A. Julia sees the moving truck outside.
   B. Julia packs up her toys.
   C. Julia leaves her old house and drives with her mom to the new house.
   D. Julia moves into her new house.

25. How does Julia feel about moving out of her old room? (RL.2.5)
   A. She's excited to move to the new house.
   B. She's nervous about leaving.
   C. She's sad about moving out of her old room.
   D. She's happy about cleaning up her toys.

> **Directions:** *Read the passage and answer the question below.*

THE GOOSE THAT LAID THE GOLDEN EGGS

There once was a man who owned a wonderful goose. Every morning, the goose laid for him a big, beautiful egg — an egg made of pure, shiny, solid gold. Every morning, the man collected golden eggs. And little by little, egg by egg, he began to grow rich. But the man wanted more.

"My goose has all those golden eggs inside her," he kept thinking. "Why not get them all at once?"

One day he couldn't wait any longer. He grabbed the goose and killed her. But there were no eggs inside her!

"Why did I do that?" the man cried. "Now there will be no more golden eggs."

END OF YEAR ASSESSMENT

FREE RESPONSE

26. How does the man react to having a goose that lays golden eggs? (RL.2.3)

_____
_____
_____
_____

> **Directions:** Read the articles and answer the questions below.

ARTICLE 1
ANIMALS OF AFRICA

Africa is home to some of the most majestic animals on Earth. Let's take a close look at some of these animals.

AFRICAN ELEPHANTS

African elephants are the largest animals on Earth that live on land. They travel in groups called herds. These herds are usually made up of related female elephants and their calves. Males normally travel by themselves. But sometimes they also form small groups with other males.

Like all elephants, African elephants have very long noses called trunks. They suck in water through their trunks and spray it over their bodies. This helps them stay cool in the heat. They also breathe and grab things with their trunks.

African elephants eat roots, grasses, fruit, and tree bark. They can eat up to 300 pounds of food in a day!

GIRAFFES

Giraffes are beautiful spotted animals. They have very long necks. They're also the tallest animals to walk the earth. Giraffes live in areas covered by grass. These areas are called grasslands.

...continued next page

Giraffes have great vision. With the help of their height and vision, they can easily spot predators, such as lions, from a distance. It's believed that other animals such as zebras form groups near giraffes for this reason. They know if danger is coming, giraffes will see it.

LIONS

Everyone knows lions are the kings of the jungle, right? Well, they don't actually live in jungles! They live in grasslands, just like giraffes. They also live in deserts.

Lions form groups called prides. Anywhere from 3 to 40 lions may live in one pride. Female lions (called lionesses) raise the cubs and hunt for food. They hunt mainly at night in small groups. Male lions defend the area where the pride is staying. They use their loud roars to scare off other animals trying to get too close.

ARTICLE 2
AFRICAN ANIMALS

Much of the continent of Africa is a savanna. A savanna is an open grassland with few trees. Africa's savanna is home to many different types of animals.

The savanna is a habitat. A habitat is a place where an animal lives. Here are some animals that live in the African savanna.

LION

Lions are big cats with gold-colored fur. Lions are carnivores (KARneh-vawrz). Carnivores are meat eaters. Lions live together in a group called a **pride**.

ELEPHANT

Elephants are animals with trunks and tusks. Elephants are herbivores (ER-beh-vawrz). Herbivores are plant eaters. Elephants live together in a group called a **herd**.

GIRAFFE

Giraffes are the tallest animals in the world. They are plant eaters. Their height helps them reach leaves on tall trees. Giraffes live in a herd of about 10 animals.

...continued next page

NAME: .... DATE: ....

END OF YEAR ASSESSMENT

Warthog

Warthogs are a type of wild hog. Warthogs are omnivores (AHM-nehvawrz). Omnivores eat both plants and meat. Female and baby warthogs live in a small group called a **sounder**. Males live alone.

Hippopotamus

Hippopotamuses are animals that live partly on land and partly in the water. They are herbivores that eat mainly grasses. Hippos live in a herd of up to 15 members.

=== **FREE RESPONSE** ===

27. What does the word *majestic* mean? (RI.2.4)

_____

_____

_____

_____

_____

28. What is the main purpose of Article 2? (RI.2.6)

_____

_____

_____

_____

_____

END OF YEAR ASSESSMENT

FILL IN THE BLANK

29. _____ is a term for animals that only eat plants. (RI.2.4)

> **Directions:** Read the words below. Choose the real-life connection that best matches the word to its use.

30. Blanket (L.2.5)
   A. sleep with   **B.** decorate   **C.** eat   **D.** walk in

31. Book (L.2.5)
   A. measure with   **B.** put in its place
   C. draw with   **D.** read

> **Directions:** Read the passage and answer the questions below.

PLAYING IT SAFE

Laura wanted to go on a bike ride, so she got her bike out of the shed and put on her pink bike helmet. Before she took off, Laura spotted her brother Tommy heading in her direction. He asked where she was going and told her he wanted to go, too. Laura invited him along for the bike ride. Tommy quickly grabbed his bike.

"Where is your helmet?" Laura asked him.

"I don't need it," Tommy answered. "I think it makes me look funny. Besides, it's uncomfortable to wear."

Laura did not think it was a good idea for Tommy to not wear his bike helmet, but she decided her brother could make his own choices. The pair started out on their bike ride ready for some adventure.

After riding for a while, Tommy said he wanted to lead the way. "Follow me!" he shouted to his sister. Laura followed Tommy down a dirt road that led them over quite a few big hills and under many tall trees. Tommy started to show off on his skills and began riding a little too fast. Slow down!" yelled Laura.

...continued next page

END OF YEAR ASSESSMENT

Tommy just ignored his sister and rode even faster. Soon he began to lose control of his bike, and he crashed! Tommy hit his leg on a big rock and bumped his head against a tree stump.

"Oh no!" cried Laura. She quickly rode over to her brother. Laura reached down and helped pull Tommy back up on his feet.

Tommy said he was very sorry. "You were right, sis," he sighed. "I guess I should have worn my bike helmet. I promise I will from now on."

TRUE OR FALSE

> **Directions:** Mark the following statements as either true or false.

32. Tommy does not speak in the story. (RL.2.6)

    A. True   **B.** False

FREE RESPONSE

> **Directions:** Write out your answers using complete sentences.

33. Why does Laura think it is not a good idea for Tommy to not wear his bike helmet? (RL.2.6)

_____

_____

_____

_____

_____

_____

END OF YEAR ASSESSMENT

> **Directions:** Read the passage and answer the questions below.

THE CLASSROOM

Ms. Jones had seven students in her classroom. Kelly, Mark, and Josh sat in the front row. Jimmy, Hannah, Claire, and Abby sat in the back row. Each morning, the students would recite the alphabet. They would write down each letter in their notebooks.

Mark liked to race through the lesson and write down the letters as fast as he could. "I'm done, Ms. Jones," called Mark.

"I see that you wrote the letters down, but some of your handwriting is sloppy. You should write them again slowly," said Ms. Jones.

While Mark was working on correcting his mistakes, Jimmy threw a paper airplane at Mark's head. Hannah giggled.

Ms. Jones looked at her students seated in the back row. "Did you do that, Hannah?" asked Ms. Jones.

Hannah suddenly stopped giggling. Her face turned bright red. "Oh no, Ms. Jones! Jimmy did it. He threw the airplane at Mark."

Jimmy hid his face behind a book.

"Is that true?" asked Ms. Jones. Claire and Abby nodded. Ms. Jones asked Jimmy to stand up. She told him he would have to go to the principal's office and explain what he had done.

Jimmy began to cry. "I'm sorry, Ms. Jones. I really am."

Ms. Jones pointed toward the classroom door. "Hurry along now, Jimmy," said Ms. Jones. Jimmy left the room and went to the principal's office. "Now let's get back to writing in our notebooks," said Ms. Jones. The students nodded their heads and began to write in their notebooks once more.

NAME: _____ DATE: _____

END OF YEAR ASSESSMENT

TRUE OR FALSE

> **Directions:** Mark the following statements as either true or false.

34. **Kelly and Josh are the only characters to not speak in the story.** (RL.2.7)
    A. True
    B. False

FREE RESPONSE

> **Directions:** Write out your answers using complete sentences.

35. **What could Jimmy have done differently to change what happened to him in the story?** (RL.2.7)

_____
_____
_____
_____
_____
_____
_____
_____
_____
_____

END OF YEAR ASSESSMENT

> **Directions:** Read the passage and answer the questions below.

1 Many people have moved to America over the centuries. Some people have ancestors who moved to America long ago. Others have relatives who moved to America more recently. Maybe someone related to you moved to America long ago. That person might have arrived at Ellis Island.

2 Ellis Island is an island in New York City's harbor. Long ago, Ellis Island was the first stop in the United States for many newcomers.

3 These newcomers were called immigrants. From 1892 to 1924, more than twelve million immigrants came through Ellis Island. Nearly all immigrants came to America by ship. They were examined at Ellis Island before they were allowed to enter the United States.

4 Many people who entered the United States through Ellis Island nicknamed it "The Island of Hope." But not everyone was allowed into the United States. Some people were turned away. They gave Ellis Island another, sadder nickname: "The Island of Tears."

5 Today, millions of people come to the United States on airplanes. Ellis Island stopped accepting immigrants many years ago. The island is now home to a museum. It tells the story of immigration. The museum shows immigrants' photographs, letters, documents, clothing, and much more. At the museum's American Family Immigration History Center, you can use a computer to see if anyone in your family came through Ellis Island.

FREE RESPONSE

36. How has the use of Ellis Island changed over time? (RI.2.3)

_____
_____
_____
_____
_____

END OF YEAR ASSESSMENT

37. How has air travel changed the use of Ellis Island? (RI.2.3)

_____

_____

_____

_____

=== FILL IN THE BLANK ===

38. Which paragraph would be the best place for a sentence about the letters you can see at the Ellis Island Museum? _____ (RI.2.2)

=== MULTIPLE CHOICE ===

39. Which paragraph teaches us about the nicknames of Ellis Island? (RI.2.2)

- **A.** Paragraph 2
- **B.** Paragraph 3
- **C.** Paragraph 4
- **D.** Paragraph 5

> **Directions:** Read the passages and answer the questions below.

THE TORTOISE AND THE HARE

One spring day, Hare was hopping through a field. Duck, Cow, Pig, and Tortoise were enjoying the sun together.

"You know," said Hare. "I have never been beaten in a race. Not once has anyone – or anything – run faster than me. Would any of you like to challenge me?"

The other animals looked at each other, none of them eager to lose a race to Hare, for Hare would never stop bragging about it. At last, Tortoise said, "I will race you, Hare. I accept your challenge."

...continued next page

"You are too funny, Tortoise," said Hare. "I could pass the finish line five times before you even start the race. Seriously, you'll be eating my dust!"

"I'll ask you to keep your bragging to yourself until the race is done," said Tortoise.

"It won't be long then. Shall we race?" asked Hare. Tortoise just nodded his head – slowly.

The other animals decided on a course. "Okay, line up," said Pig. "On your mark, get set, go!" Hare was halfway down the dusty lane before Tortoise even had his legs over the starting line.

"Slow and steady," said Tortoise. "Slow and steady."

By this time, Hare was almost to the bridge. He looked back to see if he could spot Tortoise. He wasn't sure if it was Tortoise, but there was a green and brown lump moving toward him very slowly. "My goodness," thought Hare, "I could take a nap and still win this race. Wait! I could take a nap and win." Hare curled up on the ground and, laughing to himself, fell asleep.

As Tortoise inched his way forward, Hare dreamed of running past the finish line, shaking hands with the other animals, and eating carrots. As he woke from his dream, Hare rubbed his eyes and saw Tortoise – crossing the finish line. "No!" shouted Hare. "I'm faster!"

"Slow and steady wins the race, Hare," said Tortoise with a smile. "Slow and steady."

The Town Mouse And The Country Mouse

A Town Mouse once visited a relative who lived in the country. For lunch, the Country Mouse served wheat stalks, roots, and acorns, with a dash of cold water to drink. The Town Mouse ate very sparingly, nibbling a little of this and a little of that. She was eating the simple food just to be polite.

After the meal, the friends had a long talk. The Town Mouse talked about her life in the city while the Country Mouse listened. They then went to bed in a cozy nest in the barn and slept in quiet and comfort until morning. In her sleep, the Country Mouse dreamed she was a Town Mouse. She dreamed of all the luxuries and delights of city life that her friend had described. The next day when the Town Mouse asked the Country Mouse to go home with her to the city, she gladly said yes.

...continued next page

END OF YEAR ASSESSMENT

When they reached the mansion in which the Town Mouse lived, they found on the table in the dining room the remains of a very fine meal. There were sweetmeats and jellies, pastries, and delicious cheeses. Just as the Country Mouse was about to nibble a dainty bit of pastry, she heard a Cat meow loudly and scratch at the door. In great fear the Mice scurried to a hiding place. They lay quite still for a long time, hardly daring to breathe. When they thought it was clear, they went back to the table. When they were about to eat, the door opened suddenly and a massive dog came in.

That night, the Country Mouse grabbed her belongings. "You may have luxuries that I do not have," she said to the Town Mouse as she hurried away, "but I prefer my plain food and simple life in the country with the peace and security that go with it."

FREE RESPONSE

> **Directions:** *Write out your answers using complete sentences.*

40. What is the lesson or central message in both stories? (RL.2.9)

_____

_____

_____

_____

_____

_____

41. How are the Hare and the Town Mouse alike? (RL.2.9)

_____

_____

_____

_____

_____

_____

> **Directions:** *Read the passage and answer the questions below.*

The History of the Hula Hoop

1 Have you ever played with a hula hoop? Can you keep the hula hoop up as you shake your hips? The hula hoop has been around since the mid-1900s. Two friends named Arthur Melin and Richard Knerr invented it. They were owners and creators of the company Wham-O. They made many toys in the 1900s. Their most famous toys were the hula hoop, the boomerang, and the frisbee.

2 The two owners of this company decided to make the hula hoop in 1948 when they were inspired by seeing children in other countries play with wooden hoops. They would often dance with them. Arthur Melin and Richard Knerr wanted to make a lightweight plastic hula hoop instead so kids would not get hurt and it wouldn't be too heavy for them. The creators called their new invention a hula hoop based off of hula dancing. Hula dancers from Hawaii often move their hips in a certain manner. This is the same movement needed in order to keep a hula hoop up, spinning, and off the ground.

3 The hula hoop was very popular when it first came out, but it didn't last too long like other toys. However, hula hoops are still sold today and many children own one. Some people even use the hula hoop to break records. In 2004, a winning record was achieved. A person held up a hula hoop for one hundred revelations. How long can you keep a hula hoop up?

NAME: _____   DATE: _____

END OF YEAR ASSESSMENT

=== **FREE RESPONSE** ===

42. Your teacher tells you to ask your friend a question about the article that starts with the word "why." What question do you ask your friend? (RI.2.1)

_____

_____

_____

_____

_____

_____

43. How did the creators of the hula hoop come up with the idea for this toy? (RI.2.1)

_____

_____

_____

_____

_____

_____

44. What is the main idea of this text? (RI.2.1)

_____

_____

_____

_____

_____

_____

=== **MULTIPLE CHOICE** ===

45. What was the main problem of the hula hoops from other countries? (RI.2.1)

    A. They were wooden and heavy.
    B. They were too expensive.
    C. They were old.
    D. They were metal.

ANSWER KEY

1. **Reading: Literature**
   1.1. Key Ideas and Details 186
   1.2. Craft and Structure 187
   1.3. Integration of Knowledge
        and Ideas 188
   1.4. Chapter Review 189

2. **Reading: Informational Text**
   2.1. Key Ideas and Details 190
   2.2. Craft and Structure 191
   2.3. Integration of Knowledge
        and Ideas 192
   2.4. Chapter Review 194

3. **Reading: Foundational Skills**
   3.1. Phonics and Word Recognition 195
   3.2. Chapter Review 196

4. **Writing**
   4.1. Text Types and Purposes 198
   4.2. Chapter Review 199

5. **Language**
   5.1. Conventions of Standard English ... 200
   5.2. Knowledge of Language 201
   5.3. Vocabulary Acquistion and Use 202
   5.4. Chapter Review 203

   End of Year Assessment 205

ANSWER KEY

1. READING: LITERATURE

1.1. Key Ideas and Details

1. Answer: Answers will vary
Explanation: Answers will vary but should include that the problem was solved when Ronald and his grandfather put up a fence around the turkey's nest.

2. Answer: Answers will vary
Explanation: Answers will vary but should include that they spent the afternoon building a fence because they wanted to save the baby turkeys from harm.

3. Answer: C
Explanation: Turkeys.

4. Answer: A
Explanation: Ronald and his grandfather built a fence around the turkey's nest.

5. Answer: Wilderness Camera

6. Answer: B
Explanation: Ronald wanted to spend his first day outside in his grandfather's woods.

7. Answer: Answers will vary
Explanation: Answers will vary but should include a reasonable lesson such as you should be honest so people trust you or if you break someone's trust you should try to earn it back.

8. Answer: C
Explanation: Kojo yelled "leopard" because he wanted attention.

9. Answer: Ignored him
Explanation: When he called 'leopard' for the third time the monkeys ignored him.

10. Answer: Save
Explanation: Kojo earned back the monkeys' trust by trying to save them.

11. Answer: A
Explanation: Kojo distracted the leopard because he felt guilty about lying earlier.

12. Answer: Answers will vary
Explanation: Answers will vary but should include a reasonable moral such as if you do kind things for others, people will do kind things for you.

13. Answer: Answers will vary
Explanation: Answers will vary but should include that the Lion laughed because he did not think a Mouse could do anything for a Lion.

14. Answer: Answers will vary
Explanation: Answers will vary but should include the idea that the Lion is overconfident in the beginning but learns to be more humble and rely on others.

15. Answer: Answers will vary
Explanation: Answers will vary but should include the idea that the Mouse begged to be saved and offered to help the Lion so he would not eat her.

16. Answer: B
Explanation: The Lion let the Mouse go because he was generous.

17. Answer: D
Explanation: The Mouse is not angry, the Lion is.

18. Answer: A
Explanation: The Mouse offered to help the Lion so he would not eat her.

19. Answer: Answers will vary
Explanation: When Jackie realized that Ezra did not have any Valentine's Day cards, she quickly put her bag of gifts on his desk. She let everyone know that they were from him.

ANSWER KEY

20. Answer: Answers will vary

Explanation: Answers will vary but should include that at first, Ezra put his head down on the desk and he was very sad. When Jackie gave him her gifts, he felt happy and proud.

1.2. Craft and Structure

1. Answer: A
Explanation: The student should understand what the poem is about.

2. Answer: B
Explanation: The student should know or look up the meaning of the word and discover that it means to cry or yell not "to trip."

3. Answer: A
Explanation: The student should know or look up the meaning of the words and discover that they do have similar meanings, such as "to hit."

4. Answer: A
Explanation: The student should understand that the word "twist" rhymes with "fist" based on phonemic awareness.

5. Answer: The person who was punched by Cindy is telling the poem. Answers will vary.
Explanation: The student should give examples that show that the narrator is the person who was punched ("She socked me in the stomach.").

6. Answer: Answers will vary.
Explanation: The student should explain that the author feels sorry for taking Cindy's lunch.

7. Answer: Answers will vary.
Explanation: The student will give their opinion about the title choice. (Ex: Cindy is the main character who hits the author of the poem).

8. Answer: A
Explanation: The story says that the family traveled during their spring break, which would be during March or April.

9. Answer: B
Explanation: The setting of the story is only in the airplane for the beginning of the story.

10. Answer: A
Explanation: Mason and his family packed for a four-day trip.

11. Answer: A narrator is telling the story. Answers will vary.
Explanation: The student should explain how they know that the narrator is the person who is telling the story.

12. Answer: The story begins with Mason and his family packing and flying on an airplane to NYC.
Explanation: The student should recognize this as the setting for the beginning of the story.

13. Answer: Answers will vary.
Explanation: The student should recognize that the setting changes throughout the story. They should explain that the story begins on an airplane, then changes to a hotel in NYC, the Statue of Liberty, the Empire State Building, Times Square, Central Park, and back to a hotel.

14. Answer: Answers will vary.
Explanation: The student will explain how the ending wraps up the story by having the characters talk about their vacation in their hotel room once it is over.

15. Answer: B
Explanation: The story is being told by a narrator, not Laura.

16. Answer: A
Explanation: Tommy did not practice bike safety because he did not wear his bike helmet.

1. READING: LITERATURE

ANSWER KEY

17. Answer: A
Explanation: The characters go on a bike ride, so the setting would be outside.

18. Answer: Answers will vary.
Explanation: Tommy could have worn his bike helmet or not have rode his bike so fast.

19. Answer: Answers will vary.
Explanation: The student should give their opinion. (Ex: She felt scared he would get hurt.)

20. Answer: Answers will vary.
Explanation: The student should give their opinion. (Ex: He learned his lesson after he crashed his bike and got hurt.)

1.3. Integration of Knowledge and Ideas

1. Answer: B
Explanation: Four friends are explaining and sharing their summer plans with one another.

2. Answer: D
Explanation: The student should identify that an outside narrator is telling the story.

3. Answer: A
Explanation: The word condo is short for the word condominium, which is a place to stay like a hotel or an apartment.

4. Answer: A
Explanation: Milo was slightly nervous about flying on a plane to Florida by himself.

5. Answer: A
Explanation: Milo will be swimming in the ocean and Oscar will be swimming in Lake Michigan.

6. Answer: C
Explanation: Tanya will be staying in Indiana over the summer. She will attend summer school and she will go to the Boys and Girls Club.

7. Answer: C
Explanation: Tanya will be staying in Indiana while Erica will be traveling with her dad on the semi-truck.

8. Answer: A
Explanation: The best illustration for Tanya's summer plans would be of her in the classroom because she will attend summer school.

9. Answer: B
Explanation: Oscar will spend the least amount of time in a vehicle during his summer plans because vehicles are not allowed on the island he is staying on.

10. Answer: A
Explanation: Milo is the character that will most likely spend time at the ocean because he is going to Florida.

11. Answer: D
Explanation: The student should recognize this answer as the plot of the story.

12. Answer: D
Explanation: The student should identify that a narrator is telling both stories.

13. Answer: A
Explanation: The student should recognize this as the one thing both characters did.

14. Answer: B
Explanation: Both characters saw many different underwater creatures, but both saw a fish.

15. Answer: A
Explanation: Based on the conclusion of both stories, the reader should recognize this as the correct answer.

1. READING: LITERATURE

ANSWER KEY

16. Answer: B
Explanation: Sandra had been scuba diving before so she knew how to do it; therefore, it was easier for her.

17. Answer: C
Explanation: The reader should read that Sandra went on the first day of summer, which would allow her to go again before summer ended, unlike Shane who went on the last day of the season.

18. Answer: B
Explanation: The student should recognize this as the best answer.

19. Answer: A
Explanation: If the reader compares what the two characters saw underwater, they will conclude that Sandra saw more animals and plants than Shane did.

20. Answer: B
Explanation: The student should recognize that although the two stories are not exactly the same, they are similar.

1.4. Chapter Review

1. Answer: Answers will vary.
Explanation: Answers will vary but should include that the Mouse helps the Lion by freeing him from the net he is trapped in.

2. Answer: B
Explanation: The lion is caught in the hunter's net.

3. Answer: B
Explanation: The Lion is amused because the Mouse thinks she could help a lion.

4. Answer: A
Explanation: The Mouse comes because she hears the Lion roaring.

5. Answer: B
Explanation: Because the students are learning the alphabet, this would not be a fifth-grade classroom.

6. Answer: B
Explanation: The plot of the story is that Jimmy got sent to the principal's office after throwing a paper airplane at Mark's head.

7. Answer: A
Explanation: There is Ms. Jones and her seven students.

8. Answer: A
Explanation: The illustration shows each student's seating position in the classroom.

9. Answer: D
Explanation: The poem is about a student eating lunch and seeing all the food in their lunch bag.

10. Answer: C
Explanation: The student should recognize "melted" as an adjective describing the cheese on the pizza.

11. Answer: A
Explanation: The student should recognize "green" as an adjective describing the color of the peas.

12. Answer: D
Explanation: The student should understand that the word "peas" rhymes with "cheese" based on phonemic awareness.

13. Answer: Answers will vary.
Explanation: Answers will vary but should include that the moral is not to be greedy.

14. Answer: C
Explanation: The man wanted to be rich.

15. Answer: B
Explanation: The man could have learned to appreciate what he has.

1. READING: LITERATURE

ANSWER KEY

16. Answer: Two students, Taylor and Josie both speak. The reader can tell who speaks by the use of dialogue.
Explanation: The student should understand that dialogue indicates a character is speaking. Ms. Smith has no dialogue.

17. Answer: A narrator is telling the story. Answers will vary.
Explanation: The student should identify that a narrator is telling the story and explain how they know this because the story is not told from either character's point of view.

18. Answer: Answers will vary.
Explanation: The reader should recognize that the students wanted to celebrate Earth Day so they probably were excited by the class project idea.

19. Answer: Answers will vary.
Explanation: The student will give their opinion. (Ex: They were both class leaders).

20. Answer: A
Explanation: The main characters in the first story were a Tortoise and a Hare. The main characters in the second story were Mice.

21. Answer: A
Explanation: The first story centered around a race between the main characters, but the second story did not.

22. Answer: A
Explanation: The first story ended with the Tortoise winning the race. The second story ended with the Country Mouse moving back home to the country.

23. Answer: B
Explanation: The first story had a winner in it, but the second story did not.

24. Answer: D
Explanation: Jackie gave the goody bags to Ezra because he didn't have anything to give away to his classmates.

25. Answer: Valentine's Day decorations

26. Answer: B
Explanation: Jackie saw that Ezra was really upset that he didn't have anything to give away to his classmates. If Jackie hadn't given Ezra her goody bags, then he wouldn't have anything to give to them.

27. Answer: C
Explanation: The story is about Julia and her mom moving to a new house.

28. Answer: C
Explanation: The student should know from the clues in the text that Julia is the main character.

29. Answer: B
Explanation: This is the best choice for the student to select based on the information in the text (moving truck, packing up room).

30. Answer: B
Explanation: The setting changes from Julia's old house to her new house.

2. READING: INFORMATIONAL TEXT

2.1. Key Ideas and Details

1. Answer: Answers will vary.
Explanation: Answers will vary but should include that the main topic of the passage is how oranges go from the tree to your house.

2. Answer: Answers will vary.
Explanation: Answers will vary but should include that oranges are checked by computer.

ANSWER KEY

3. Answer: Packing Plant
Explanation: Oranges are cleaned and packaged at a packing plant.

4. Answer: Warm
Explanation: Oranges grow in places with warm weather.

5. Answer: Picker
Explanation: The picker removes oranges from trees.

6. Answer: A
Explanation: When oranges arrive at the packing plant they are put on a machine with moving rollers.

7. Answer: A
Explanation: Paragraph six is about how oranges move from stores to people's homes.

8. Answer: B
Explanation: The next step after picking an orange is transporting it to a packing plant.

9. Answer: Answers will vary.
Explanation: Answers will vary but should include that tornadoes happen in Kansas because it has the right weather conditions and lots of open space.

10. Answer: Answers will vary.
Explanation: Answers will vary but should include that tornadoes start as thunderstorms.

11. Answer: Answers will vary.
Explanation: Answers will vary but should include that the passage is about what tornadoes do, how they form, and how they are tracked.

12. Answer: A
Explanation: Radar can tell us how fast a tornado is moving.

13. Answer: B
Explanation: Tornadoes do not move very quickly. We can use radar to predict where they will go.

14. Answer: A
Explanation: A tornado warning means that a tornado has touched down.

15. Answer: A
Explanation: This sentence tells about the storm in Greensburg. It should go in paragraph 1.

16. Answer: D
Explanation: The main idea is that the warning system saved lives.

17. Answer: Answers will vary.
Explanation: Answers will vary but should include that the creators of the hula hoop came up with the idea after seeing children from other countries dance with a wooden hoop.

18. Answer: Answers will vary.
Explanation: Answers will vary but should include that the creators came up with the name hula hoop from hula dancing in Hawaii.

19. Answer: Answers will vary.
Explanation: Answers will vary but should include that the main idea is to explain how people break records using hula hoops.

20. Answer: A
Explanation: Arthur Melin and Richard Knerr created the company Wham-O.

2. 2. Craft and Structure

1. Answer: Answers will vary.
Explanation: Satellites are in the Earth's orbit. They have many jobs like tracking the weather and giving signals to cell phones.

ANSWER KEY

2. READING: INFORMATIONAL TEXT

2. Answer: Answers will vary.
Explanation: The term orbit means the path of one space object around another.

3. Answer: Debris
Explanation: The junk in space is called debris.

4. Answer: Satellites
Explanation: The Hubble Space Telescope and International Space Station are both satellites.

5. Answer: C
Explanation: Article 1 iis to teach readers about satellites and the important work they do.

6. Answer: B
Explanation: Article 2 is to teach readers about space debri sand the possible problems it can cause.

7. Answer: Answers will vary.
Explanation: The Grover loved school, but he had to quit. His father died when he was young and he had to quit school in order to support his mother and siblings.

8. Answer: Answers will vary.
Explanation: Answers will vary but should include The author can use the title "Unique President" due to the fact that Grover Cleveland was the 22nd and the 24th president of the United States.

9. Answer: B
Explanation: The author is trying to explain interesting facts about President Grover Cleveland.

10. Answer: D
Explanation: Grover Cleveland dropped out of school because he had to get a job to support his family.

11. Answer: 22nd and 24th

12. Answer: Helping Native Americans gain back their land

13. Answer: Answers will vary.
Explanation: Answers will vary but should include that a national park is an area of land that is protected from people who want to cut down its trees or hunt the animals living in it.

14. Answer: Answers will vary.
Explanation: Answers will vary but should include that the purpose of the text is to teach us about Canaima National Park.

15. Answer: Answers will vary.
Explanation: Answers will vary but should include a reasonable reason for the author to teach us about the park.

16. Answer: Answers will vary.
Explanation: Answers will vary but should include that tepuis are mountains with flat tops.

17. Answer: Answers will vary.
Explanation: Answers will vary but should include that endangered animals are in danger of going extinct.

18. Answer: C
Explanation: The author is describing the Appalachian Mountains.

19. Answer: A
Explanation: The Appalachian Mountains are in the United States and Canada.

20. Answer: B
Explanation: Tourists can hike the Appalachian Trail when they visit the Appalachian Mountains.

2. 3. Integration of Knowledge & Ideas

1. Answer: Answers will vary.
Explanation: Answers will vary but should include that Article 1 is about satellites and Article 2 is about space debris.

ANSWER KEY

2. Answer: Answers will vary.
Explanation: In the first article, the author discusses the subject of satellites and their purpose. In Article 2, the author explains how parts of broken satellites make up space debris. The author also explains how if not handled properly, space debris can break existing satellites.

3. Answer: Answers will vary.
Explanation: The author of Article 2 supports the claim that space debris is a problem by explaining how it gets in the way of satellites and breaks them.

4. Answer: A
Explanation: Article 1 gives more information about different satellites.

5. Answer: Answers will vary.
Explanation: The author supports the point that President Grover Cleveland was a unique president because he served two terms as president. However, he did not serve these terms together. No other president has done this. This makes Grover Cleveland unique.

6. Answer: Answers will vary.
Explanation: Answers will vary but should include that one article says giraffes live in the savanna and the other says they live in grasslands. However, the savanna is grasslands so they are both talking about the same place.

7. Answer: Answers will vary.
Explanation: Answers will vary but should include a fact that is in both articles, such as elephants live in herds.

8. Answer: Answers will vary.
Explanation: Answers will vary but should include an important fact that is in Article 2 but not in Article 1, such as which type of eater each animal is.

9. Answer: Answers will vary.
Explanation: Answers will vary but should include that the author gives details about giraffes such as them being tall, spotted, and with a long neck.

10. Answer: 1
Explanation: Article 1 talks about how giraffes stay stay safe from predators.

11. Answer: B
Explanation: It would be better to read Article 2 because it is about more different types of animals.

12. Answer: Answers will vary.
Explanation: Answers will vary but should include that the Earthquakes are dangerous and are caused when tectonic plates hit each other.

13. Answer: Answers will vary.
Explanation: In article 2, the author explains the most powerful earthquake in the world and the damage it caused.

14. Answer: Answers will vary.
Explanation: Article 1 explains more information about tectonic plates and the layers of the Earth.

15. Answer: A
Explanation: quickly

16. Answer: A
Explanation: Article 1 has more information about tectonic plates.

17. Answer: A
Explanation: Earthquakes are not rare and happen frequently. Many occur and people are usually unaware of them.

18. Answer: 2
Explanation: Article 2 tells how often earthquakes happen.

19. Answer: A
Explanation: The quote "Scientists know this due to the type of rocks that make up the mountains" supports the fact that the Appalachian Mountains is the oldest mountain range in the United States.

ANSWER KEY

20. Answer: B
Explanation: The purpose of the text is to teach us about the Rocky Mountains.

2.4. Chapter Review

1. Answer: Answers will vary.
Explanation: Answers will vary but should include that the environment for a tornado occurs during a tornado watch and a tornado warning.

2. Answer: Answers will vary.
Explanation: Answers will vary but should include a question "When should people take shelter?"

3. Answer: Answers will vary.
Explanation: Answers will vary but should include that tornadoes occur when warm wet air meets with cool, dry air.

4. Answer: Answers will vary.
Explanation: Answers will vary but should include that explains what a tornado is and how it occurs.

5. Answer: 4
Explanation: Paragraph 4 tells about tornado alley.

6. Answer: 5
Explanation: Paragraph 5 tells about how tornadoes are tracked and how people are warned about them.

7. Answer:
Explanation: Kansas was the setting for the movie The Wizard of Oz, and a tornado occurred in the movie.

8. Answer: Meteorologists
Explanation: Meteorologists use radar to track storms.

9. Answer: 8
Explanation: 8 states are in Tornado Alley.

10. Answer: A
Explanation: Radar can tell us how fast a tornado is moving.

11. Answer: B
Explanation: Tornadoes move very slowly so it is easy for meteorologists to tell where they will go and when they will hit.

12. Answer: A
Explanation: Paragraph one explains a real tornado that was dangerous to a small town.

13. Answer: Answers will vary.
Explanation: Answers will vary but should include that the purpose of the text is to teach us about Elizabeth Blackwell, the first woman doctor.

14. Answer: Answers will vary.
Explanation: Answers will vary but should include that the author supports the claim by telling how Elizabeth continued to pursue her dream of being a doctor and then helped others get health care and become doctors.

15. Answer: Answers will vary.
Explanation: Answers will vary but should include that the author wanted us to learn about a strong woman from history.

16. Answer: Answers will vary.
Explanation: Answers will vary but should include that Elizabeth started a school for women, which gave women a place to get medical training.

17. Answer: C
Explanation: She worked hard by continuing to pursue medical school even though the schools did not accept women.

18. Answer: Answers will vary.
Explanation: Answers will vary but should include that the author is explaining how power is divided between three branches of the US government.

ANSWER KEY

19. Answer: Answers will vary.

Explanation: Answers will vary but should include that branches of government to the three parts the federal government is broken up into (legislative, executive and judicial).

20. Answer: C

Explanation: In this context branches means parts.

21. Answer: D

Explanation: The purpose of the article is to teach us how power is divided among the three branches.

22. Answer: Justices

Explanation: Justices are people who serve on the Supreme Court.

23. Answer: A

Explanation: The president's cabinet is his group of advisors.

24. Answer: Answers will vary.

Explanation: Answers will vary but should include that both articles are about the memorial that was built for Dr. King.

25. Answer: Answers will vary.

Explanation: Answers will vary but should include that the author of Article 1 wants to explain that a memorial was built for Dr. King and teach us about a ceremony that happened to mark the start of construction.

26. Answer: Answers will vary.

Explanation: Answers will vary but should include that Article 1 focuses are the start of construction. Article 2 focuses on the memorial and how it was paid for.

27. Answer: Answers will vary.

Explanation: Answers will vary but should include that Article 1 focuses are the start of construction. Article 2 focuses on the memorial and how it was paid for.

28. Answer: Answers will vary.

Explanation: Answers will vary but should include that a memorial is a statue or a place that honors a person or an event.

29. Answer: Answers will vary.

Explanation: Answers will vary but should include that Article 2 is about the memorial to Dr. King, what it looks like, and a concert that helped raise money for it.

30. Answer: Answers will vary.

Explanation: Answers will vary but should include that the author is showing us that only very important people have memorials on the Mall.

3. READING: FOUNDATIONAL SKILLS

3.1. Phonics and Word Recognition

1. Answer: B

Explanation: The "o" vowel makes a long "o" sound.

2. Answer: B

Explanation: The teacher, Mr. Adams, told the students they were going on a field trip to the museum.

3. Answer: A

Explanation: The "u" vowel makes a short "u" sound.

4. Answer: B

Explanation: The word park has a short "a" sound.

5. Answer: D

Explanation: The student should understand that they should look up words they do not know the meaning of.

ANSWER KEY

6. Answer: B
Explanation: The "o" vowel makes a long "o" sound.

7. Answer: C
Explanation: The card had a code number on it that the student would use during their visit.

8. Answer: D
Explanation: The code number gave the student more information about the items in the museum.

9. Answer: C
Explanation: The vowel team for the word tried is "ie".

10. Answer: C
Explanation: The vowel team for the word throat is "oa".

11. Answer: A
Explanation: The student should understand that the song lyrics are sung at a baseball game using the words in the song as a clue (ball game).

12. Answer: B
Explanation: The student should understand that the song is not asking a question but making a command.

13. Answer: A
Explanation: The vowel team for the word peanuts is "ea".

14. Answer: A
Explanation: The student should understand that the song lyrics are asking for someone to buy peanuts and cracker jack.

15. Answer: B
Explanation: The student should understand that if they do not know a word or what something is, they should stop reading and look it up or mark it to look up later.

16. Answer: A
Explanation: The student should know the meaning of the word or look it up.

17. Answer: B
Explanation: The vowel team for the word team is "ea".

18. Answer: A
Explanation: The student should recognize this is true from the song lyrics.

19. Answer: B
Explanation: The student should know the meaning of the word or look it up.

20. Answer: A
Explanation: Pausing can add effect or expression when counting. The student should not read them as regular words without emphasizing them.

3.2. Chapter Review

1. Answer: B
Explanation: The word *blast* has the short /a/ sound.

2. Answer: C
Explanation: The word *time* has the long /i/ sound.

3. Answer: A
Explanation: The word *rainy* has the long /a/ sound. The vowel blend *ai* makes the long /a/ sound in this word.

4. Answer: B
Explanation: The word *throat* has the long /o/ sound. The vowel blend *oa* makes the long /o/ sound in this word.

5. Answer: D
Explanation: The consonant /s/ can make different sounds. In the words *visit* and *desert* the letter *s* makes the /z/ sound.

ANSWER KEY

6. Answer: B
Explanation: The word *people* has an irregular spelling. Irregularly spelled words have letters that make an unusual sound. In the word *people*, the vowel blend *eo* makes the long /e/ sound.

7. Answer: A
Explanation: The suffix -ful means "full of." The word *careful* best completes in this sentence.

8. Answer: again
Explanation: The word *again* has an irregular spelling. Irregularly spelled words have letters that make an unusual sound. In the word *again*, the vowel blend *ai* makes the short /e/ sound.

9. Answer: show, row
Explanation: The vowel blend *ow* can make different sounds. In the words *show* and *row* the letters *ow* make the long /o/ sound.

10. Answer: unkind
Explanation: The prefix un- means "not."

11. Answer: grumbled
Explanation: The student should know that this is the only two-syllable word.

12. Answer: nothing or beyond
Explanation: The student should know that these are the only two-syllable words.

13. Answer: camera
Explanation: The student should write the misspelled word correctly.

14. Answer: daddy
Explanation: The student should understand that "he" represents daddy in the poem.

15. Answer: Answers will vary.
Explanation: The student will come up with another word similar to crawling (Ex: digging).

16. Answer: shak/ing
Explanation: The word shaking has two syllables and should be broken up this way to show each syllable in the word.

17. Answer: sound/ed
Explanation: The word sounded has two syllables and should be broken up this way to show each syllable in the word.

18. Answer: quacking
Explanation: The poem says, "And the ducks all quacked as if they were daft."

19. Answer: re/spond
Explanation: The word respond has two syllables and should be broken up this way to show each syllable in the word.

20. Answer: WHEN
Explanation: The student should understand that words in all capital letters signal to the reader that they should be emphasized or shouted.

21. Answer: grizzly; Answers will vary.
Explanation: Example: The grizzly bear quickly ran across the woods.

22. Answer: Answers will vary.
Explanation: The student should acknowledge that the bears are quite large. They are tall and can weigh up to 800 pounds. It would be surprising that such a large animal can move so fast.

23. Answer: prefix; Answers will vary.
Explanation: Example: He can decode the secret language for us.

24. Answer: suffix; Answers will vary.
Explanation: Example: The little girl was full of goodness.

25. Answer: Answers will vary.
Explanation: The student can say that grizzly bears live in North America, they can be found in forests and meadows, they can also be seen in woodlands and prairies.

3. READING: FOUNDATIONAL SKILLS

Some live in Yellowstone. Many live along rivers and streams.

26. Answer: Answers will vary.
Explanation: The student can say that grizzly bears use sounds, smells, scratch, or use body language to talk to each other.

27. Answer: Answers will vary.
Explanation: The student should recognize that the word pairs are closely spelled but pronounced differently. They will come up with word pairs of their own (Ex: beep, jeep).

28. Answer: Answers will vary.
Explanation: The student should recognize that the word pairs are closely spelled but pronounced differently. They will come up with word pairs of their own (Ex: bright, delight).

29. Answer: Answers will vary.
Explanation: dive; five; hive; live

30. Answer: Answers will vary.
Explanation: The student should understand from the text that hibernation is a deep sleep that animals go into for five to eight months. They sleep day and night and hide from the cold snow.

4. WRITING

4.1. Text Types and Purposes

1. Answer: B
Explanation: The author's opinion is that stores should separate toys by gender.

2. Answer: C
Explanation: The sentence "It makes a store more organized" best supports the author's opinion.

3. Answer: B
Explanation: This sentence uses a linking word.

where to find it" uses a linking word to connect opinions and reasons. The word *if* is a linking word in this sentence.

4. Answer: A
Explanation: The sentence "I think sweets should be banned from school because they aren't good for children" best describes the author's opinion.

5. Answer: C
Explanation: The sentence "Bake sales are popular" does not support the author's opinion.

6. Answer: C
Explanation: The word *but* acts as a linking word in this sentence. Linking words connect ideas.

7. Answer: D
Explanation: The sentence "India is in South Asia" best introduces the topic of this text.

8. Answer: B
Explanation: The sentence "India is home to many different animals" is a fact.

9. Answer: A
Explanation: The sentence "That means it has water on three sides" is a definition.

10. Answer: A
Explanation: This statement is true. This sentence gives details about the character's actions and feelings.

11. Answer: B
Explanation: This statement is false. This sentence does not give details about the character's actions and feelings.

12. Answer: A
Explanation: This statement is true. This sentence uses the temporal word *then* to show event order.

ANSWER KEY

13. Answer: A

Explanation: The word *suddenly* is a temporal word in this sentence. Temporal words connect ideas and show transitions.

14. Answer: B

Explanation: The sentence "The day was warm, and the sky was china blue" does not describe the character's actions.

15. Answer: D

Explanation: First Daisy caught sight of the butterfly, the she crouched down to take a closer look.

16. Answer: C

Explanation: The sentence "She sat by the lake and wondered" does not use any temporal words. Temporal words connect ideas and show transitions.

17. Answer: Answers will vary.

Explanation: Students should be able to write a narrative conclusion that provides a sense of closure.

18. Answer: Linking

Explanation: The underlined word is an example of a linking word in the text.

19. Answer: Opinion

Explanation: This sentence states the author's opinion about spring.

20. Answer: Answers will vary.

Explanation: Students should demonstrate an understanding of how to end an opinion piece with a concluding statement.

4.2. Chapter Review

1. Answer: C

Explanation: The sentence "A cere is the skin above a parakeet's beak" is a definition.

2. Answer: D

Explanation: The sentence "A parakeet is a type of bird" best introduces the topic of this text.

3. Answer: A

Explanation: The sentence "Overall, parakeets can be chatty birds" best concludes this text.

4. Answer: B

Explanation: The sentence "Parakeets are interesting" is an opinion, not a fact.

5. Answer: A

Explanation: This statement is true. The words *and, also,* and *because* are examples of linking words.

6. Answer: A

Explanation: This statement is true. The words *finally, before* and *later* are examples of temporal words.

7. Answer: B

Explanation: This statement is false. Opinion writing is not based on facts about a topic.

8. Answer: B

Explanation: This statement is false. Informative texts present information. Narratives should tell a story.

9. Answer: C

Explanation: The sentence "Slow lorises live in the rainforest" is a fact.

10. Answer: D

Explanation: The sentence "They are taken from their homes" does not use a linking word.

11. Answer: A

Explanation: This statement is true. The author most likely has a positive opinion about slow lorises.

ANSWER KEY

12. Answer: A
Explanation: This statement is true. The author likely has a negative opinion about keeping lorises as pets.

13. Answer: B
Explanation: The sentence "But lorises are not meant to be pets" best describes the author's opinion.

14. Answer: D
Explanation: All of these sentences support the author's opinion.

15. Answer: B
Explanation: The sentence "She thinks lorises are in danger of dying out" expresses someone else's opinion.

16. Answer: C
Explanation: The sentence "In conclusion, lorises are cute but do not make good pets" would best conclude this text.

17. Answer: Topic
Explanation: Oymakon is the topic of this passage.

18. Answer: Fact
Explanation: This sentence is a fact used to develop the topic of the text.

19. Answer: Definition
Explanation: This sentence is a definition used to develop the topic of the text.

20. Answer: A
Explanation: "Solar eclipses happen every twenty five years"

21. Answer: B
Explanation: "The solar eclipse happens when the sun, moon, and Earth align"

22. Answer: C
Explanation: The sentences "Did you see it then? It was so cool to see!" is not a fact like the other sentences.

23. Answer: A
Explanation: The best concluding statement would be "So, mark your calendars for 2042 and get your solar eclipse glasses!"

24. Answer: A
Explanation: The sentence "He didn't want to be embarrassed" best describes the character's feelings in the text.

25. Answer: B
Explanation: The sentence "Scot opened his bookbag, got out his math notebook, and opened it up to homework he did last week" best describes the character's actions in the text.

26. Answer: B
Explanation: The sentence "Then, the bell ran" has a transition that shows event order.

27. Answer: B
Explanation: The sentence "She really wanted to look nice and impress the judges because one portion of the score is rider and horse presentation" describes the character's thoughts in the text.

28. Answer: A
Explanation: The story describes a detailed sequence of events in order.

29. Answer: B
Explanation: This story does describe the character's actions during her horse riding competition.

30. Answer: B
Explanation: The topic of this text is the history of writing stories.

5. LANGUAGE

5.1. Conventions of Standard English

1. Answer: B
Explanation: A group of elephants is called a herd.

ANSWER KEY

2. Answer: C
Explanation: A group of people is called a group.

3. Answer: B
Explanation: The student should recognize that don't is the correct placement for the apostrophe.

4. Answer: C
Explanation: The student should recognize that she'll is the correct placement for the apostrophe.

5. Answer: B
Explanation: The correct contraction for will not is won't.

6. Answer: C
Explanation: The correct contraction for cannot is can't.

7. Answer: C
Explanation: The correct contraction for I am is I'm.

8. Answer: D
Explanation: The plural form of foot is feet.

9. Answer: D
Explanation: The plural form of tooth is teeth.

10. Answer: B
Explanation: The correct reflexive pronoun is myself because the subject of the sentence is "I".

11. Answer: A
Explanation: The correct reflexive pronoun is ourselves because the subject of the sentence is "we".

12. Answer: B
Explanation: The past tense form of sit is sat.

13. Answer: B
Explanation: The correct adverb is carefully to describe placed.

14. Answer: D
Explanation: Badge is the correct spelling.

15. Answer: D
Explanation: Flavor is the correct spelling.

16. Answer: Bright, red, fast
Explanation: The student should recognize bright, red, and fast as adjectives.

17. Answer: Rocky
Explanation: The student should recognize rocky as an adjective.

18. Answer: Timothy, Nike
Explanation: The student should recognize the formal name and brand should be capitalized.

19. Answer: Halloween, October
Explanation: The student should recognize the holiday and month should be capitalized.

20. Answer: Texas, Florida
Explanation: The student should recognize the states should be capitalized.

5.2. Knowledge of Language

1. Answer: B
Explanation: This is not formal English. It is not proper to address people as "girl".

2. Answer: A
Explanation: This is informal English to address someone as "dude."

3. Answer: B
Explanation: This is a formal, not informal, question.

4. Answer: B
Explanation: This is not formal English. It is not proper to begin a sentence with "Yo."

5. LANGUAGE

www.prepaze.com   Copyrighted Material

ANSWER KEY

5. Answer: A
Explanation: This question is written in formal English.

6. Answer: A
Explanation: This is an informal English sentence with the abbreviation "LOL" and the extended word "sooo."

7. Answer: B
Explanation: This is not an informal question.

8. Answer: A
Explanation: Yes, all papers written in school as assignments for your teacher should use formal English and its conventions.

9. Answer: A
Explanation: Formal English should be used when speaking to an authority figure.

10. Answer: B
Explanation: There are times when informal English can be written such as when texting a friend.

11. Answer: A
Explanation: The first sentence is the only choice that uses formal English.

12. Answer: D
Explanation: The last sentence is the only choice that uses informal English.

13. Answer: A
Explanation: The first sentence is the only choice that uses informal English.

14. Answer: C
Explanation: The third sentence is the only choice that uses formal English.

15. Answer: A
Explanation: Formal and informal English can be used on the phone to speak with family and friends.

16. Answer: C
Explanation: We use formal English to write and speak properly and informal English when communicating with people we know in a comfortable setting.

17. Answer: Answers will vary.
Explanation: Hello! Let's go before we are late.

18. Answer: Answers will vary.
Explanation: What is going on?

19. Answer: Answers will vary.
Explanation: Hey! Can ya hear me?

20. Answer: Answers will vary.
Explanation: Yo! Like where are we all going?

5.3. Vocabulary Acquistion and Use

1. Answer: B
Explanation: The closest definition for the word "imagine" is to dream.

2. Answer: C
Explanation: The closest definition for the word "appearance" is look.

3. Answer: B
Explanation: The closest definition for the word "incorrect" is wrong.

4. Answer: C
Explanation: The closest definition for the word "misspoke" is spoke wrong or incorrectly.

5. Answer: B
Explanation: The real-life use for an umbrella is to keep dry from the rain.

6. Answer: D
Explanation: The real-life use of an orange is to eat.

ANSWER KEY

7. Answer: B
Explanation: The real-life use shoes is to walk in.

8. Answer: A
Explanation: Based on the provided definition, the word "additional" means to add on or something that is extra.

9. Answer: D
Explanation: Based on the provided definition, the word "careless" means to be thoughtless or have little care.

10. Answer: D
Explanation: An apple is not a spicy food.

11. Answer: C
Explanation: Corn is not a juicy food.

12. Answer: A
Explanation: The provided definition for "birdhouse" is correct.

13. Answer: B
Explanation: The provided definition for "lighthouse" is incorrect. A lighthouse is a navigational symbol used to guide sailors at night.

14. Answer: A
Explanation: The provided definition for "ridiculous" is correct.

15. Answer: B
Explanation: The provided definition for "diagram" is incorrect. A diagram is a chart.

16. Answer: A
Explanation: The verb "toss" describes the category *to throw*.

17. Answer: A
Explanation: The verb "pitch" describes the category *to throw*.

18. Answer: A
Explanation: The verb "capture" describes the category *to catch*.

19. Answer: B
Explanation: The adjective "slim" does not describe the category *thick*.

20. Answer: A
Explanation: The adjective "scrawny" describes the category *thin*.

5.4. Chapter Review

1. Answer: D
Explanation: A group of wolves is called a pack.

2. Answer: C
Explanation: The real-life use of a pencil is to draw with.

3. Answer: B
Explanation: The real-life use for a desk is to write on.

4. Answer: A
Explanation: The real-life use a song is to sing.

5. Answer: A
Explanation: The closest definition for the word "cautiously" is carefully.

6. Answer: B
Explanation: The closest definition for the word "rescue" is to save.

7. Answer: A
Explanation: The closest definition for the word "dislike" is to not like or don't like.

8. Answer: C
Explanation: The plural form of child is children.

9. Answer: C
Explanation: The correct reflexive pronoun is themselves because the subject of the sentence is "they."

5. LANGUAGE

www.prepaze.com Copyrighted Material

ANSWER KEY

10. Answer: C
Explanation: The student should recognize that Smith's is the correct placement for the apostrophe.

11. Answer: A
Explanation: The student should recognize that couldn't is the correct placement for the apostrophe.

12. Answer: D
Explanation: The correct contraction for we will is we'll.

13. Answer: C
Explanation: Based on the provided definition, the word "posttest" means a test taken after a lesson or a final test.

14. Answer: A
Explanation: Based on the provided definition, the word "disagree" means to not agree or approve of something.

15. Answer: C
Explanation: The past tense form of hide is hid.

16. Answer: B
Explanation: The past tense form of tell is told.

17. Answer: C
Explanation: The correct adverb is evenly to describe spread.

18. Answer: A
Explanation: The correct adverb is quickly to describe ran.

19. Answer: A
Explanation: Craft is the correct spelling.

20. Answer: C
Explanation: Sweep is the correct spelling.

21. Answer: A
Explanation: The adjective "chunky" describes the category *thick*.

22. Answer: B
Explanation: The adjective "bulky" does not describe the category *thin*.

23. Answer: A
Explanation: The provided definition for "triumph" is correct.

24. Answer: B
Explanation: The provided definition for "origin" is incorrect. An origin is the beginning of something.

25. Answer: B
Explanation: The verb "drop" does not describe the category *to throw*.

26. Answer: A
Explanation: The verb "grab" describes the category *to catch*.

27. Answer: B
Explanation: The verb "fling" does not describe the category *to catch*.

28. Answer: Caramel, sweet, creamy
Explanation: The student should recognize caramel, sweet, and creamy as adjectives.

29. Answer: McDonald's
Explanation: The student should recognize the restaurant name should be capitalized.

30. Answer: California, Disneyland
Explanation: The student should recognize the state and theme park should be capitalized.

ANSWER KEY

END OF YEAR ASSESSMENT

1. Answer: C
Explanation: The sentence "This made books very beautiful" is an opinion, not a fact.

2. Answer: D
Explanation: All of these sentences are explanatory.

3. Answer: Answers will vary.
Explanation: Answers will vary but should include that Uncle Joseph was telling Eric that the time machine could go to places more interesting than yesterday.

4. Answer: Brontosaurus
Explanation: Eric and his uncle see a Brontosaurus.

5. Answer: Answers will vary.
Explanation: Answers will vary but should include that the main purpose of this text is to explain the role of a potter and a particular potter named Jody Narango.

6. Answer: A
Explanation: "She plans to teach poetry to her daughters" best supports the author's claim that Jody Naranjo wants to keep the tradition going.

7. Answer: C
Explanation: The sentence "Another invention changed bookmaking about 550 years ago" best introduces the topic of this text.

8. Answer: A
Explanation: The sentence "It made books a treasure everyone could enjoy" is a concluding statement in this text.

9. Answer: B
Explanation: A good opinion piece does include reasons to support the writer's opinion.

10. Answer: A
Explanation: A writer can use linking words to connect opinions and reasons.

11. Answer: B
Explanation: A group of seagulls is called a flock.

12. Answer: A
Explanation: The plural form of mouse is mice.

13. Answer: D
Explanation: This is the only descriptive phrase that is not used to describe the milk in the poem.

14. Answer: B
Explanation: The student should understand that the word "silly" rhymes with "Billy" based on phonemic awareness.

15. Answer: St. Louis, Missouri
Explanation: The student should recognize the city and state should be capitalized.

16. Answer: Easter, March, April
Explanation: The student should recognize the holiday and months should be capitalized.

17. Answer: Answers will vary.
Explanation: The dodo bird became extinct by explaining the two reasons it became extinct. The dodo bird became extinct from predators and because citizens hunted them and ate them.

18. Answer: Answers will vary.
Explanation: The lesson of the story is to get your work done and not to waste your time.

19. Answer: Winter
Explanation: The ants spent the summer getting ready for winter.

20. Answer: A
Explanation: Article 1 tells when construction on the King Memorial started.

ANSWER KEY

21. Answer: 2
Explanation: Article 2 tells how the King Memorial was paid for.

22. Answer: C
Explanation: The closest definition of the word "unhappy" is sad.

23. Answer: A
Explanation: The provided definition for "bookshelf" is correct.

24. Answer: C
Explanation: In the middle of the story, the characters are moving from their old house to their new house.

25. Answer: C
Explanation: The student should understand that Julia is sad because she lets out a sigh, a tear runs down her cheek, and she stands in the middle of her empty room remembering the fun times she had there, signaling to the reader that she is crying and sad.

26. Answer: Answers will vary.
Explanation: Answers will vary but should include that the man became greedy and wanted all of the golden eggs.

27. Answer: Answers will vary.
Explanation: Answers will vary but should include that majestic means powerful or great.

28. Answer: Answers will vary.
Explanation: Answers will vary but should include that the purpose of Article 2 is to teach about some of the animals that live in the savanna in Africa.

29. Answer: Herbivores
Explanation: Herbivores only eat plants.

30. Answer: A
Explanation: The real-life use of a blanket is to sleep with.

31. Answer: D
Explanation: The real-life use of a book is to read.

32. Answer: B
Explanation: Tommy has dialogs in the passage.

33. Answer: Answers will vary.
Explanation: The student should say something about how Tommy could get hurt by not wearing his bike helmet.

34. Answer: A
Explanation: Kelly and Josh have no dialogue in the story.

35. Answer: Answers will vary.
Explanation: Jimmy could have not thrown the paper airplane at Mark's head.

36. Answer: Answers will vary.
Explanation: Answers will vary but should include that Ellis Island has changed from an immigration center to a museum.

37. Answer: Answers will vary.
Explanation: Answers will vary but should include that air travel ended the use of Ellis Island because people now fly into the country instead of arriving on boats that pass Ellis Island.

38. Answer: 3
Explanation: Paragraph 3 is about things you can see at the museum, it would be the best place for this sentence.

39. Answer: C
Explanation: Paragraph 4 is about the nicknames for Ellis Island.

40. Answer: Answers will vary.
Explanation: The lesson or central message in both stories is that you need to believe in yourself and your own life.

ANSWER KEY

41. Answer: Answers will vary.
Explanation: The Hare and the Town Mouse were over confident.

42. Answer: Answers will vary.
Explanation: Why did the creators of Wham-O create the hula hoop?

43. Answer: Answers will vary.
Explanation: They came up with the idea to design a hula hoop when they saw children from other countries dancing with a wooden hoop.

44. Answer: Answers will vary.
Explanation: The maid idea of this text is that the creators of Wham-O designed and created plastic hula hoops.

45. Answer: A
Explanation: The main problem of the hula hoops from other countries were that they were wooden and heavy.

REFERENCES CITED

- *A Tricky Monkey,* by ReadWorks
- *Building A Better Bicycle,* by ReadWorks
- *Canaima National Park,* by ReadWorks
- *Chirping Chirp,* by ReadWorks
- *Countries of the World,* by National Geographic Kids
- *Daddy Fell into the Pond,* by Alfred Noyes
- Excerpt from *"Daisy Dawson is on Her Way",* by Steve Voake
- *Goodbye, Bake Sales?,* by Time for Kids
- *Helping Our Planet,* by Sara Peters
- *Honoring a Great American,* by ReadWorks
- *In Memory of Dr. King,* Written by ReadWorks
- *Keeping Traditions Alive,* by ReadWorks
- *Should Stores Separate Toys by Gender?,* Written by Time for Kids
- *Slow Lorises are Being Stolen from the Rainforest,* by National Geographic Kids
- *Spinning Storms,* by ReadWorks
- *Take Me Out to the Ball Game,* by Jack Norworth
- *The Ants and the Grasshopper,* by Aesop's Fables
- *The Classroom,* by Sara Peters
- *The First American Woman Doctor,* by ReadWorks
- *The Goose That Laid the Golden Eggs,* from ReadWorks
- *The Heron and the Hummingbird,* by A Native American Folktale
- *The Lion and the Mouse,* by Aesop's Fables

REFERENCES CITED

- *The Miniature World of Marvin and James,* by Elise Broach
- *The Power of the Earth,* by ReadWorks
- *The Rocky Mountains,* by ReadWorks
- *"The Story of Books",* by Cricket Media
- *The Terrible Thing About Cindy,* by Barbara Vance
- *The Three Branches of Government,* by ReadWorks
- *The Time Machine,* Written by ReadWorks
- *The Tortoise and the Hare,* Written by Aesop's Fables
- *The Yo-Yo,* by ReadWorks
- *What is it Like to Live in the Coldest Town Known to Man?,* by The Washington Post
- *What is the United Nations?,* by ReadWorks
- *Why Are There Earthquakes?,* by ReadWorks

Made in the USA
Las Vegas, NV
10 November 2020